To K

So 1

know you

You are one of the

greats!

Dottie Walters

The Greatest Speakers
I Ever Heard

THE GREATEST SPEAKERS I EVER HEARD

DOTTIE WALTERS

WRS
PUBLISHING

A Division of WRS Group, Inc.
Waco, Texas

First published in the United States of America in 1995 by WRS Publishing, A Division of WRS Group, Inc., 701 N. New Road, Waco, Texas 76710
Book design by Colleen Robishaw
Jacket design by Joe James

10 9 8 7 6 5 4 3 2 1

Library of Congress Cataloging-in-Publication Data

Walters, Dottie.
    The greatest speakers I ever heard / Dottie Walters.
      P.   cm.
    Includes index.
    ISBN 1-56796-052-9 : $19.95
    1. Orators--United States--Biography. I. Title.
PN4057.W35 1994
815.009--dc20
    [B]   94-19657
                                                                  CIP

This book is dedicated to Audrey Lohr, my secretary,
who worked by my side through every step of the work.
With great appreciation.

Acknowledgment of Photographs

All photographs in this book are courtesy of Sharing Ideas Newsmagazine *for professional speakers. They were published as part of articles and interviews with the speaker and publisher, Dottie Walters. Three exceptions are the photograph of Bishop Sheen published herein courtesy of Sheen Productions, 23 East Main Street, Victor, New York 14564; the photograph of Napoleon Hill, published here courtesy of the Napoleon Hill Foundation, 1440 Paddock Drive, Northbrook, Illinois 60062; the photograph of Aimee Semple McPherson published in this book courtesy Rolf K. McPherson, D.D., President Emeritus, International Church of the Foursquare Gospel, 1910 West Sunset Boulevard, Los Angeles, California 90026.*

Table of Contents

Cavett Robert
Attorney at Law, Chairman Emeritus and Founder,
National Speakers Association
The soul and the spirit of that organization

Foreword

I met Dottie Walters at the first meeting of the National Speakers Association in Phoenix, Arizona. Dottie had been speaking around the world, prior to that time. I can say without reservation, that I feel her fabulous *Sharing Ideas Newsmagazine* about the world of paid speaking has impact, brilliance, useful ideas, and is framed in humor and entertainment.

She helps so many people. I have never had a telephone call or letter from her that she was not trying to do something to help another person.

My worldwide speaking career began when I was just five years old, when they asked me to speak at a large family wedding. My uncle said, "If you'll get up and give a speech while we are waiting for the bride and groom, I'll give you a nickel!" That was the beginning of a long career of paid speaking.

I began as a young attorney practicing in New York. There I met Ralph Smedley (founder of Toastmasters International) who gave me courage about my fear of appearing on the platform. Ralph said, "Cavett, if you don't have a fear of speaking you'll never be any good! You'll be too casual and come across as though you don't care."

So I thought, maybe it's a good thing that I'm frightened!

Tom Dewey, who was in charge of racket investigations, gave me a job as an investigator. He asked us to work "just half a day—I don't care which twelve hours." My health broke down, so I moved to Arizona where the climate is dry. There I met Senator Barry Goldwater and John Hammond, the impresario, and began my speaking career in earnest. Today I often share the platform with my lovely daughter, Lee.

Dottie has asked me to tell you about the speaker who had the greatest personal impact on my life. That man was Will Rogers. Will often said, "Don't let yesterday take up too much of today. The world is full of cactus, but we don't have to sit on it." I heard Will Rogers make the last speech he ever made on this earth. Shortly thereafter he and Wiley Post started their flight around the world and met with a fatal accident in Alaska.

The occasion was a small dinner party in August 1935. Will Rogers began his speech thus, "I don't know what you folks do for a living, but please take my advice: You can't heat an oven with snowballs."

Will Rogers went on to say, "You must use the firewood of knowledge, love, and belief. You gotta know what's cooking, you gotta love what's cooking, you gotta BELIEVE in what's cooking. Success is just as simple as that."

He exemplified the greatness of simplicity. Will starred in four moving pictures, wrote fifty-two weekly newspaper columns and fifty-two weekly radio shows, and delivered one hundred and fifty professional speeches each year. Will walked with kings, yet "never lost the common touch" as Rudyard Kipling said.

I am proud that Dottie Walters has been chosen by WRS Publishing to write this book about the greatest speakers she has ever heard. What a line-up of the greats! I have known many of them personally and have spoken on the same platform with them. I know you will love this book.

With Dottie Walters' speakers bureau, books, audio albums, speeches, and *Sharing Ideas Newsmagazine,* she has touched many lives. If service to others is the rent we pay for the space we occupy on this earth, Dottie Walters' rent is prepaid from now on through eternity.

—*Cavett Robert*
Chairman Emeritus, National Speakers Association

Introduction

"Walking the tightwire is living:
everything else is waiting."

—Karl Wallenda, famous tightrope walker

Dottie Walters was a depression child, born in Los Angeles, California, who lost her home several times. By the time she entered high school, her father had left her mother and her permanently. Dottie went to work in a midnight bakery every day after school and every weekend. She was the only breadwinner.

Her high school English teacher insisted she take journalism. After Dottie washed the bakery cases and mopped the floors, it became very quiet in the open-to-the-street midnight market. Dottie took out paper bakery bags, leaned on the counter, and wrote poems, editorials, stories, articles, and even a make-believe advice-to-the-lovelorn column (this last under the *nom de plume* of Professor O.G. Whataline) for her beloved Alhambra High School Moor. Soon she also took over the duties of advertising manager. The day after graduation Dottie got two full-time jobs, one of which was on the *Los Angeles Times*.

That summer she realized her friends were leaving for college and that there was no way she could go. Dottie had always haunted the library and was an avid reader. She determined not to be uneducated. She has read at least six books every week of her life, mainly autobiographies, and today, many trade journals as well.

Dottie and Bob Walters, who returned from the bloody battles of the South Pacific with the 2nd Marine Division, were married, had two children, bought a small tract home and a dry cleaning business. Then recession hit. Determined to help her husband and resolved that her children should not lose their home, Dottie began a tiny advertising business on foot, pushing her two babies in a broken-down baby stroller in rural Baldwin Park.

She traded baby-sitting with her neighbor and borrowed the neighbor's car to speak to service clubs about customer service. She placed a copy of the *Baldwin Park Bulletin* with her advertising shopper's column marked with green crayon at each luncheon place.

The merchants asked her to start her own advertising business. She built that business into four offices, 285 employees, and four thousand continuous-contract advertising accounts. At the same time, her speaking grew into a second profession and led her to podiums around the world.

Dottie sold this large advertising business to concentrate on her own speaking, writing, the administration of her speakers bureau, Walters International, and the publishing of her top international magazine for speakers, speakers bureau owners, and meeting planners, *Sharing Ideas Newsmagazine.*

Dottie Walters has spoken in the U.K., South Africa, the United States, Canada, Australia, Japan, Malaysia, and Singapore. She is a professional consultant and writes books and articles for many international publications. Dottie has been interviewed on CNN, ABC, "Good Morning Australia," "Good Morning South Africa," and hundreds of other TV programs, as well as thousands of radio shows. She has been interviewed by newspapers and magazines worldwide and is featured on American Airlines' Business Channel on all domestic and international flights. Dottie has her own daily "Good Business" radio show, which is heard on one hundred national radio stations via the Business Radio Network.

Dottie has created many world famous audio albums on sales and the world of paid speaking. She is a founding member and past national board member of the National Speakers Association and is the organizer and founder of the bureau association, The International Group of Agencies & Bureaus.

She has not only spoken on the same platform as many of the speakers in this book, she has personally known them, interviewed them in her *Sharing Ideas Newsmagazine,* and often booked them through her speakers bureau. In her professional lifetime she has heard a tremendous parade of famous speakers. In this book, Dottie Walters shares her insider comments, thoughts, and personal impressions of "The Greatest Speakers I Ever Heard."

Chapter 1

*"A great speaker is first a great person
who happens to speak well."*

—Aristotle

In gathering these stories of the great speakers I have had the privilege to hear and know, I hope to inspire you to recall those who inspired, influenced and captivated you with their words, delivery, and most of all—with their ideas and lives.

I asked my friend John Morley, famous foreign press correspondent who has interviewed every world leader for the past forty years, "What is the one trait they all have in common?" John told me, "Dottie, the one thing they shared is that they were all gifted speakers. Some used their gift for evil, some for good."

The world remembers and cherishes the great speakers. Speaker Don Hutson tells about hearing the beloved Dr. Kenneth McFarland close a speech by admiring the beautiful new auditorium where the program was presented. Dr. McFarland brought the audience to its feet as he spoke about great speakers of the past, "Jesus of Nazareth never had the luxury of a microphone, or an auditorium like this—he spoke in the fields."

Traveling in time

Thinking of the great speakers in my personal and professional life, I also think of those in ages past who are remembered, but were never recorded. Let's visualize H.G. Wells' Time Machine. Will you climb aboard with me to travel back to Nazareth to hear Jesus speak by the sea? Perhaps then we will truly understand why the Roman soldier in the audience remarked, "Never a man so spake!"

Then let's fly to France. My friend of the mind Ben Franklin often reads his letters aloud in the evening to his influential French friends who gather to discuss strategy. What Ben says persuades France to arm General Washington and send Lafayette and his troops to aid America. Let's join his small audience. Listen.

Ben is reading his letter to George Washington, who is discouraged and disheartened. His troops are freezing and starving at Valley Forge. George has written, "Is anybody there? Does anybody care?"

"Don't be downhearted, George," Ben says. "If you could see yourself as we see you, every mile of distance we are apart is like a year. From here, we see the great leader you truly are, fighting to begin the first country in the world based on democracy and freedom. The world of the future will salute you, as we in France do now."

Let's slip into the back of the Continental Congress in America and hear Ben Franklin speak to the Thirteen Colonies. His speech sets their resolve to put aside bickering and differences. Because of Ben, they vote to make one nation of the United States. Without his speech, our country might have died aborning. Notice, it is not only Ben's words, or even his content that matters, it is his magnificent spirit and persona that move their hearts. Look at their faces. They recognize him.

Voices in the books

It was at the library that I met him, my dear friend of the mind, Ben Franklin. In struggling to begin my tiny advertising business with no college education or car, I read all the business books in the small Baldwin Park Public Library. One was by the popular sales speaker, Frank Bettger, *How I Raised Myself from Failure to Success Through Selling*. All through the book, Frank told me about his personal inspiration, Ben Franklin. I took Frank Bettger back to the library, found Ben Franklin's autobiography and fell in love with Ben's great mind, delightful humor, scientific inquiring ideas, and brilliant strategy. When you come to visit my office in Glendora, California, you will see Ben's pictures, statues, and hundreds of books by and about him which I keep close to me. I have a big life size photograph of the famous Houdan bust where I can see him now. I often think, how would Ben handle this problem? He always gives me sound advice and then he winks at me and grins! Oh yes, it is true. Ben loves women. (We love him back.)

Someone kindly gave me an audio tape recorded by an actor who read Ben Franklin's autobiography. I only listened to it a little while. (You see, it was not his voice.)

Curtain up!

Aboard our time machine, let's join the audience as Aesop tells his story of the fox who jumps at delicious grapes of opportunity, but gives up very quickly, saying, oh, well, those grapes are probably sour, anyway. Master storyteller Aesop illustrated his story. Look, he holds up a bunch of grapes as a prop! At the back of the room he has his stories written on scrolls, available at the speaker autograph table.

Aesop's lessons are just as valuable today. Most of us give up far too easily. To be victorious, we must not complain of sour grapes. Those who grasp Aesop's point determine instead to take jumping lessons.

Let's watch Diogenes hold up his prop, a lighted lamp. He tells his audience the story of his dramatic search for honesty.

We won't want to miss hearing the motivational Demosthenes. They said of him: "When others speak, we applaud. But upon hearing Demosthenes, we rise and go to war!" Was it practicing with pebbles in his mouth that made Demosthenes great? It helped his pronunciation, but it was his ability to make a point, and illustrate it with a magnificent story, that set the audience on fire. Great speakers create stories which flash with drama in the theater of each listener's mind. Such stories reside in our hearts forever… generation after generation.

A speech is remembered because of the way it moves us. Let's join the sad crowd standing before Robert Emmet, the Irish patriot, and then across the ocean, America's Nathan Hale. Each speaks from the gallows about freedom.

They left the same message, "I only regret I have but one life to give for my country."

Before we talk together of more modern speakers, let's slip into the crowd and hear St. Francis of Assisi give his beautiful talk, "Lord let me be a channel of Your love. Where there is hatred, let me sow love."

Come join the audience listening to Thomas Traherne in England. The year is 1637. Listen to this speech:

> *"You never enjoy the world aright,*
> *'till the sea itself flows in your veins,*
> *'till you are clothed with the heavens,*
> *and covered with the stars.*
> *And perceive yourself to be the sole heir of the whole*
> *world and more than so,*
> *because people are in it who are every one sole heirs*
> *as well as you.*
>
> *'Till you can sing and rejoice and delight in God,*
> *as misers do in gold, and kings in scepters,*
> *then within you flow the seas of life, like wine."*

Hear that pounding? It's Martin Luther nailing up his proclamation on the church door. He speaks to the waiting crowd, "Here I stand!" He personifies Aristotle's "great person, who happens to speak well."

Do you wish, as I do, that you could have been there the day his modern namesake, Martin Luther King, gave his earth-moving "I Have a Dream!" speech? Thank goodness his words were recorded and are available to us.

The power voice

Great speakers have an aura about them. Caesar's legions called after him, "There goes our leader! He is never discouraged!" We who have been in business very long know that everyone gets discouraged sometimes. Especially the leader. No one is exempt. Caesar never let his men know when his spirit burned low. His voice rings with courage, power, and enthusiasm. He knows discouragement is endemic. Caesar reminds me of Vince Lombardi, the magnificent football coach who said to his audiences, "In the heart of each player is a dream and a hurt. I *never* speak of hurts. If I did, the player would concentrate on the injury. Instead I focus on the dream. Then the player sees it too, recovers, and rises to become a champion."

It was Jack Dempsey, world champion boxer, who told his audiences, "A Champion is the one who gets up. Even when he can't."

First speakers bureau

English author/speaker Charles Dickens inspired the start of the very first American speakers bureau in Boston, The Redpath Lyceum Bureau. A speakers bureau is an independent business which books speakers for their clients' programs. Charles Dickens complained that he could not find one in this country. Dickens always sold thousands of his books at the back of the auditorium. (We call it BOR today—back-of-room sales.) Charles Redpath heard him, acted upon the ancient advice "Carpe diem!" (seize the day) and built a huge organization with offices in many U.S. cities.

My Scottish grandfather, Robert Soutter of the clan McFarland, loved Charles Dickens, who was as famous for speaking as he was for writing.

In running our Walters International Speakers Bureau with fax machines and computers, I often think of Charles Redpath and his staff, who wrote their speaker booking contracts in longhand. Redpath had no phones or electricity, and yet booked the most famous and dynamic speakers of the post Civil War period. Among them was the spiritual Ralph Waldo Emerson (who insisted that "oats for horse" be added to his speaking contract); Clara Barton who founded the Red Cross; Dorothea Dix who spoke for reform of hospitals for the insane; and many others.

Charles Redpath took the famous Chautauqua speakers out on the road in "circuits" to outlying cities along the new railroad lines. P.T. Barnum spoke for Redpath on "How to Make Money." Mark Twain delighted audiences with his wit and sold many books. Many women spoke on the platforms of the Chautauqua. Lucy Snow and Susan B. Anthony's subjects were antislavery and women's rights. Mary E. Lease was called the "Joan of Arc of Kansas." Frederick Douglass and Sojourner Truth, who rescued so many from slavery and led them north, were magnificent black abolitionist speakers.

Before we leave the Chautauqua, we don't want to miss hearing the world champion of all their speakers, William Jennings Bryan, who presented his powerful "Cross of Gold" speech. He was paid fifteen hundred dollars per program, a fortune in those times.

It was another prolific author, the great speaker Dr. Charles Spurgeon of London, England, who inspired my Scottish Grandpa to come to America with a pack on his back at age eighteen. Like every truly great speaker I have ever known, Dr. Spurgeon lived his philosophy. He helped people in every way he could. I have the letter Dr. Spurgeon wrote for my Grandpa in 1880, recommending him to "any American employer who needs a bright and hard working young man." It is framed and on the wall of our offices. Grandpa carried Dr. Spurgeon's letter with him all of his life. I hope "bright and hard working" might describe my life, too.

Who turned you on?

When you ask your friends which speaker meant the most in their lives, they pause, raise their heads, and remember. Then a smile lights their eyes and they say, "Ah, yes. I recall hearing _____ tell a story about _____. It lifted me out of my seat! It changed the course of my life."

Great speakers affect their audiences in astounding ways. I believe this is because the great speaker flashes a light of recognition into our minds. We suddenly see a truth that was already there. Like a hunting dog puppy who points his tail back, and his nose forward, when he first sees a bird. He recognizes it. The instinct awakens.

The ideas great speakers present are like a mirror flashing a bright signal from a far-off power source. We are transfixed. We have been waiting for that very message. We already knew it. We recognize it. We say to ourselves, "This is *true*. This is the confirmation I have been waiting for. I recognize it and welcome it like the electrifying sight of our nation's flag in a foreign land."

In choosing the great speakers for this book, I have researched the lives of those who are gone, and have asked the ones I work with today who lit the fire in their hearts. The link—from speakers, to audience members, who then become speakers themselves—is absolutely fascinating!

I have shared the platform with great speakers all over the world, and worked with them in our speakers bureau. I know thousands of them. I recall not only the content of their programs and their magnetic delivery, but also the kind of person they are off-stage. Do they "walk their talk?" Do they live up to the advice they give others? The great ones I have chosen to tell you about certainly do.

Fanny Brice, the original "Funny Girl" said, "Let the world know you as you are, not as you think you should be. Sooner or later, if you are posing, you will forget the pose, and then where are you?"

In talking to you about the great speakers, we will look at the total person. I share with you little things I remember, endearing things about each speaker that reveal the person they are.

Come with me now. I will tell you stories of the great speakers, their messages, their lives, and those great speakers who inspired THEM!

Norman Vincent Peale
World-beloved speaker, author of
The Power of Positive Speaking

Chapter 2

Dr. Norman Vincent Peale

When we in the business of booking speakers say a speaker "walks the walk, and talks the talk," we mean the person is genuine. Sincere. The speaker does not just give lip service to the subject. The speaker lives it every day, reflecting in every action who he is. Such a man was Dr. Norman Vincent Peale. His magnificent book, *The Power of Positive Thinking* (Prentice Hall), has profoundly influenced people all over the world.

It was when I had proudly purchased my very first business cards for my tiny advertising business that I first heard Dr. Peale speak. I was thrilled when my neighbor bought two tickets and invited me to go with her to hear him. The Pasadena Civic Auditorium was filled to overflowing. The story Dr. Peale told which impressed me most that day was the one about how he started *Guideposts* magazine. This glorious inspirational publication is filled with positive real-life stories, one of my favorite spirit lifters.

Most of us presume that great things jump to life, adult and complete, like Venus rising from the sea. I had no idea that Dr. Peale struggled to begin *Guideposts*. That day he told us about his early difficulties and triumphs. To start the magazine, Dr. and Mrs. Peale gained the support of Frank Gannett, founder of the Gannett newspaper chain; J. Howard Pew, the Philadelphia industrialist; and Branch Rickey of the Brooklyn Dodgers. Together they raised twelve hundred dollars to start *Guideposts*.

They worked out of a rented room over a grocery store in Pawling, New York. The first issue contained a single story by World War II flying ace and magnificent speaker, Captain Eddie Rickenbacker.

When fire destroyed their office and their list of subscribers, a broadcast by Lowell Thomas, famous newscaster and electric speaker, opened a floodgate of help. Dr. Peale wrote over thirty books, created many inspirational audio cassettes, and wrote for newspapers and magazines. He was a world famous and most beloved speaker. When I heard him tell of the early struggles of *Guideposts*, I understood. I knew exactly how it is to begin with nothing and fight the good fight to pay the bills, no matter what.

After Dr. Peale's program, I wanted to shake his hand, as hundreds did, and to thank him for his magnificent message. I pulled one of my precious new business cards from my purse, and handed it to him. Maybe he saw the pride in my eyes. He knew that a business card is the personification of the person and their work. That small piece of cardboard symbolized for me the hard-won little advertising business I was very proud of. It represented not only a way to save our home, but it was a triumph over the words of my father before he left my mother and me. He had said I was not worth educating.

Dr. Peale took my card that day and carefully put it in his pocket. I was so pleased that he kept it. Two days later, the mail came to my office bearing an envelope with Dr. Peale's name on the return address. I was so excited! Inside was a handwritten note. Dr. Peale said, "Dottie, I am proud of you and your business." I wept.

How many people gave Dr. Peale their business cards that day? How many hours did he spend writing to all of us? Dr. Peale walks the talk.

Dr. Peale reminds me of my high school journalism teacher. I always thought I was her pet. She loved everything I wrote. Later I met other students from that same class. Each confessed confidentially, "Did you know that I was her pet?"

She had love enough for each of us. Like the mother of sixteen who was asked how she could have enough love for so many? She explained, "You misunderstand the nature of love. Love cannot be divided. Only multiplied."

My business grew and grew. About two years later a writer called me to ask if she could write the story of how I began for a magazine—Dr. Peale's *Guideposts*! Of course I was delighted. They titled it, "What Can One Housewife Do?" Under my picture they captioned, "Dottie Walters is the author of a new book, *Never Underestimate the Selling Power of a Woman*."

There were no books for women in sales then. I read my way around the Baldwin Park Library consuming every book about sales, management, and business. But there was a coldness in my heart as I realized in the midst of each book that the author never mentioned a woman as the boss, the salesperson, or as the customer with the ability to buy without a husband or father's help. In those days only five percent of our United States sales force were women. All of the books about sales talked of men as the salesperson, the buyer, manager, manufacturer. Women were only spoken of as "spouse."

I wanted to help the women who were starting in sales, as I was. The advice for men often just did not fit us. But, I had not been able to sell my book to a publisher. Eighteen of them turned down my manuscript. So the book mentioned in *Guideposts* was unpublished. A dream.

Then one day the phone rang. It was Dr. Peale! He said he had told my story of starting a business on foot, pushing two babies in that rickety stroller, in many of his programs. He wanted to inform his audiences about the publisher of my book so that they could buy it. I gulped.

I confessed that I had been turned down by every major publisher because they felt there was no interest in books for women in sales.

Dr. Peale said, "I will help you."

He called his publisher, then phoned back to tell me, "The man who stood in your way at my publisher's has just retired. Try again."

That book is now in the fifteenth edition and is sold all over the world. At this writing, fifty-five percent of the sales force in the United States are women. Women are starting thousands upon thousands of businesses. Maybe they got tired of hitting their heads on the glass ceilings of corporations. Maybe they delight in having their very own business cards printed with the words, President, CEO, or Manager on them. I am so grateful that Dr. Peale helped me to give them a hand up the ladder.

We asked Dr. Peale when he began speaking. He told us he started when he was just seventeen years old, when

Kenneth McFarland
Eloquent Spokesman for General Motors,
winner, Freedom Foundations Award

he spoke in every county in Ohio to the Boy's Congress. He was inspired to speak when he heard the magnificent orator William Jennings Bryan, in Brooklyn, New York.

Dr. Peale noticed that Bryan was a master of the pause. He would stop after making a magnificent point, pour a glass of water, letting the audience think over his message, then drink very slowly. Then he would turn and continue. Bryan was a passionate speaker who believed fervently in what he said.

Our dear friend Dr. Peale was called home on Christmas Eve, 1993. He was ninety-five years young. Every moment of his life was spent helping people, encouraging them, believing in them. He never wasted a moment.

What rejoicing there must have been on the other side for this man who gave hope, love, and new life to all the world. While we all miss him terribly, I feel as the "Queen Mum" of England did when she said about the death of George VI. "We must feel gratitude for what has been, rather than grief for what is lost."

Dr. Norman Vincent Peale is not gone. All his great ideas and his love are with us still.

Dr. Kenneth McFarland

William Jennings Bryan inspired another great speaker, Dr. Kenneth McFarland. Bryan had a dynamic and powerful voice. People who came to hear other Chautauqua speakers on village greens along the railroad lines left their speakers' audiences and moved over to join Bryan's at the first sound of his voice. To give you an idea of his content here is a marvelous quotation by Bryan, a favorite of speaker W Mitchell, "The Man Who Would Not Be Defeated." (W Mitchell is paralyzed from the waist down and very badly burned over most of his body.) "Destiny is not a matter of chance: It is a matter of choice. It is not a thing to be waited for: It is a thing to be achieved." —William Jennings Bryan.

If you were to ask most of the speakers in the United States who are over forty years of age to list their most beloved speakers, they would include Dr. Kenneth McFarland. He was the superintendent of schools in

Topeka, Kansas, and spokesperson for General Motors. Like all other great speakers, Dr. McFarland told stories in the most wonderful way. You could see the scene he described in every detail. He never needed any electronic overhead projectors. He used the power of magnificent words, beautiful delivery, and complete sincerity.

Since my family are of the Clan McFarland, Ken and I often joked that we both are "of that ilk" as they say in Scotland. I often told my children, "A great positive solution is waiting for us. Let's find it!" From the time they were little, I taught them to take their own pulse when they had a scrape or a bump. They stopped crying and got busy finding the beat in their wrist. Then I hummed, "Scotland, the Brave" to them, and told them their pulse said, "Here come the bagpipes playing Scotland, the Brave! Get up! Get UP! GET UP!"

Ken was known as the nation's most eloquent and effective exponent of the American free enterprise system. He was the recipient of the Freedom Foundation's prestigious National Leadership Award. When Freedom Foundation's President Kenneth Wells presented their plaque and Exemplar Medal to Dr. McFarland at Valley Forge, he said, "I shall identify our Freedom Leadership Award winner with a simple unqualified statement: Dr. Ken McFarland is the greatest public speaker in the United States today."

Dr. McFarland wrote wonderful letters of encouragement to me as I struggled with my advertising business and began my speaking career—as he wrote to thousands of others who loved him. When I asked him to author the foreword for one of my books, he complied at once, and told the story of his daughter, who is a judge. He was very proud of her.

Dr. McFarland was inspired to become a speaker, as Dr. Norman Vincent Peale was, by the same speaker—the famous William Jennings Bryan. Here is the story Ken often told from the platform, to the delight of his audiences.

His mother saved her pennies for a long time to buy one of the first victrolas, and to accompany it, William Jennings Bryan's very popular "Cross of Gold" speech on a record.

She played that record over and over for her family. Ken felt William Jennings Bryan's inspirational ideas were part of his family. Then one day something wonderful happened. Young Ken heard that Bryan was coming to town to speak for the Chautauqua. Ken determined to meet Bryan in person.

It was a sweltering hot day at the railroad station. Young Ken McFarland was dressed in his usual "summer ensemble." A pair of overalls. Nothing else. Barefoot. Ken came in hopes of at least catching a glimpse of the great orator.

Bryan stepped down off the train onto the platform—dressed splendidly, a great contrast to the country boy. This poem came into my mind as I heard Ken McFarland tell the story. He projected the scene vividly in the theater of my mind. I wrote it on the back of the program that day:

"A poor boy stood by a big puffing train
With his worn overalls, and his feet just plain.
Up strode the man who had come to speak
Dressed all in velvet, his cigar oblique.
He strutted and pranced. Bryan knew he was great!
Checked his gold watch (speech never late).
The little boy watched him, followed close behind.
Bryan strode stately. Gave him no never-mind.
William Jennings Bryan was a powerful man.
Silly kid couldn't matter to his mighty plan.
Suddenly he turned! Almost tripped on the boy.
Kid's eyes lighted with amazing joy!
Big man stopped. Saw something there.
"Hey, why you here? Did you take a dare?"
"My Mama saved her money, buyed a victrol'r.
Plays your "Cross of Gold! Sir, when I'm older..."
The boy hesitated. "Son, you got a PLAN?
Tell me what you'll be, when you're grown a man!"
Bryan reached out. Their eyes were locked.
If they only knew it, the world just rocked!
Far in the future, all across the nations

Red Motley
Renowned sales speaker, chairman of the board,
Parade Magazine

Audiences stood—in wild ovations.
"Son, what's your dream? Come, take my hand."
"Yes! I'll speak like you!" said Ken McFarland.

Red Motley

My husband found a job in industrial tool sales. The Sales and Marketing Club of Los Angeles brought in great speakers to inspire the sales people who worked for the big companies who were their members. My Bob is always very encouraging to me. When his boss said his company had purchased tickets for all of their sales people, Bob asked if he might buy an extra one and take me along. The event was held at the Shrine Auditorium, which seats several thousand people.

One of the fine speakers that night was the publisher of *Parade Magazine*, Red Motley. Parade is inserted in thousands of U.S. Sunday newspapers. His power point was that nothing happens in our economy until "somebody sells something."

Red told us of traveling cross country via trains to call on customers, before the days of flying. Because I was hiring and training saleswomen in my advertising business, I was particularly interested in his story of how he taught his staff to think first, last, and always of their customer's interest.

"If it is cold and snowing, leave your overcoat with the secretary." He said, "Don't bring a wet coat into the customer's inner office, then fumble around looking for a place to park it. Never smoke in the customer's office, even if you are invited to. Every moment you spend on a cigarette is a moment you are not concentrating on the customer's needs."

Red reminded me of a football coach. I had never heard a person who ran such a large business talk about training people before. I learned that he would not put up with sloppy work, poor appearance, lack of interest or creativity. Red was tough.

Not long after that I picked up a woman to train in advertising sales in the Palm Springs area. I always kept my car radio on, to listen for ads about new businesses. Sure enough, an elaborate new gas station and auto repair center was opening at the just finished Smoke Tree Center. I told my trainee that I had waited to buy gas so that we could do so at the new station. We would call on the owner while we were there. She said: "If he is using radio advertising, why would he want to spend more money with you?"

I thought, "Now Dottie, give her a chance." As we drove to the gas station I explained that people who advertise are always the best prospects for more advertising, and that this rule applies in selling anything. I turned into the gas station. She commented, "Well, the owner certainly won't be here. He has better things to do. This is ridiculous."

We stopped at the pump. A man with a lovely smile beamed at us. I asked, "Is the owner of this magnificent new facility here today?" He answered, "Yes! I am the owner!"

I grinned back at him and asked him to fill up my tank and check the oil. Then I nudged my trainee with my elbow and said: "Get out. Smile. Don't say anything. Just watch me make this sale while he fills my tank and takes care of my engine."

As I grabbed my briefcase, she replied, "If you think I'm going to degrade myself by standing on this hot asphalt, you have another think coming."

I got out, closed the sale, picked up the new owner's check, shook hands, and got back into the car. "When will you start my training?" my recruit whined.

I thought of Red Motley and drove her home. Three strikes and you're out. Red Motley taught me to be tough like he was and to invest my time with good people. I will never forget him. Since I never had a sales manager, I "adopted" Red and often thought how he would handle sales training. One day the muse grabbed me and I wrote these words for my sales staff:

Remember the words of Red Motley?

"We gotta sell goods to somebody.
Nothing's going to happen until we're done.

Commerce begins when the contract's won!"
I'm in SALES where I like to be!
Business and industry count on me.
Factories hum. Ships set sail.
Truckers roll out. Checks hit the mail.
I'm in SALES where I want to be
Trading and barter rely on me.
I WRITE THE ORDERS. The world turns 'round.
Shopping centers open. Jobs abound.
I'm in SALES where I love to be!
You can take welfare, dump it in the sea.
I fill needs, so enterprise can be
Free to do business! Depend on me!

Sometimes women forget what it was like to be a woman in business just a few years ago. The Sales & Marketing Executives invited anyone in the audience who employed sales people to come forward at the intermission to pick up an application for membership and to leave their business card. By this time, I had over one hundred sales people on my staff. The night we heard Red Motley, I ran down in front, and bang! The glass ceiling crashed right on my head.

The officials handed my card back. "Why?" I asked. "I am qualified!"

"We don't allow women in our organization," they told me sternly. "It does not matter how qualified you are." Is there anything more hurtful than rejection?

However, no one could stop the tide of women who were determined to succeed in business. I was glad to hear that Sales & Marketing opened their doors to everyone just a few years later, as did Toastmasters, Kiwanis, Lions Club, Rotary, and many others.

Bill Gove

My husband took me and our son Mike, who had just started high school, to another of the Sales & Marketing

Bill Gove
First president, National Speakers Association,
recipient Toastmasters' Golden Gavel Award

Executive meetings. The speaker that night was Bill Gove. Bill completed his B.A. degree by attending seven years of night classes at the Boston University, then began his career with the 3M Company. Bill was such an outstanding sales speaker for his company, he went out on his own and has presented over five thousand programs. Toastmasters International presented its prestigious Golden Gavel Award and Sales & Marketing Executives bestowed its Distinguished Speaker Award to him. Bill served as the first president of the National Speakers Association.

A remarkable thing happened to our son Mike that night. His grades had not been the best. He didn't know what he wanted to do with his life. One of Bill Gove's stories was that his own career took a change for the better when he realized that he was not responsible for the people in his audience. They might heckle him, someone might be drunk. But how they acted was their own responsibility. They would receive the results of their own actions. No one escapes.

Bill explained he was responsible *to* his audience. He must always do his best, no matter what. That was the important thing. Our Mike decided that night to go on to college. He is now an attorney in Rancho Bernardo, California. (He and his lovely wife, Diane, are both attorneys/speakers/authors.) We are very grateful to Bill Gove for that message at the auditorium in Los Angeles.

It was my pleasure recently to sponsor one of Bill Gove's seminars in our town of Glendora. I asked him which speaker had inspired him. He said, "It was Dr. Kenneth McFarland, Dottie." Bill's favorite quote is by Albert Einstein: "Aging is not a fixed biological process. It is any number of perceptions made real by collective agreement."

Come and travel into the theater of the mind in our next chapter, and let me introduce you to more great and exciting speakers: Charles Roth, Amelia Earhart, and Bruce Barton.

Aimee Semple McPherson

Dramatic speaker whose church fed, housed and
clothed more Los Angeles residents than any
other organization during the depression

Chapter 3

My First Great Speaker

It was a Sunday night in Los Angeles. As we entered the giant auditorium, they handed us a clothespin. I believe I was about three and a half years old. I remember holding my mother's hand as we went into the large beautiful building, Angelus Temple, located across from Echo Park.

Each person in the row had hold of a length of clothesline rope. It stretched from one end of the long line of seats all the way to the other end. I was so small that my mother put the thick seat up and let me sit on the top edge so that I could see. My feet dangled far from the floor.

Up in the front of the building I saw three long lines of what appeared to be ocean waves made of painted cardboard. At each end of the waves were men holding handles. Later they moved them back and forth to simulate ocean waves. This was before the days of TV, so you can imagine my curiosity about the waves, clothespins, and the clothesline.

Then on the stage we saw a white lifeboat on wheels. Standing in the front was a majestic figure—a beautiful blonde woman in a white nurse's uniform with a navy blue, crimson-lined cape around her shoulders.

The music soared. She led us in singing an old hymn, "Throw out the lifeline, throw out the lifeline, some poor sinner is drowning tonight!" The waves moved up and down.

I will never forget her voice. She spoke with power and passion. Loud, then soft. I saw each scene in my mind and visualized each character as she acted out her stories. She explained that her mission was the "Salvation Navy." She told about how many families Angelus Temple was feeding, helping, housing, and clothing in that terrible depression.

The props she used—music, boat, and moving waves—were to help the audience see the scenes she described so vividly. She was a master storyteller/impresario. I remember thinking, "she does not need the boat or the waves. I see the stormy sea here in this big room! I see the homeless, hungry people. We must help them!"

Aimee Semple McPherson was one of the most successful speakers in American history. Her mother was a soldier in the Salvation Army. Aimee began her speaking career addressing crowds from the running board of her old Packard car, then in tents, boxing rings, bars, and finally in the established churches of her time. Actor Charlie Chaplin gave her ideas about the sets she used for her illustrated sermons at Angelus Temple. In her band was a young man named Anthony Quinn. He played sax.

More people came to hear her speak than ever saw the magician Houdini or attended P.T. Barnum's circus. The church she established, the International Church of the Foursquare Gospel, had 410 branches when she died, with two hundred mission stations. Under the leadership of her son Rolf McPherson, this church today has 25,577 churches in seventy-four countries.

On that long ago Sunday evening, this little girl remembers that when it was time for the collection, Sister Aimee asked everyone in the audience of five thousand to take out their folding money and pin it to their "lifeline" rope with their clothespin.Thus we all "threw out the lifeline." My mother let me pin our dollar to the clothesline. How I hoped it would help those poor homeless people. I understood how they felt.

That night I heard my first great speaker. A living legend.

"O Hope! Dazzling, radiant Hope!
What a change thou bringest to the hopeless,
brightening the darkened paths, and cheering the
lonely way."

—*Aimee Semple McPherson*

Bruce Barton

The first great speaker I met and spoke to personally was Bruce Barton, the founding father of American advertising, president of Batten, Barton, Durstine & Osborn. When I met him, I needed his knowledge badly.

My husband and I had purchased a small tract home in rural Baldwin Park, California. My husband needed my help in the recession. We were about to lose the small business he had started, as well as our home. I had lost my home several times as a child. My mother and I walked the streets at night. I looked into the windows of lighted houses and wished I could go home. I was determined that our children would not experience that agony.

The story of how I started my tiny advertising business is in the introduction of this book. As I worked at selling ads, I was afraid that the newspaper publisher and my advertising customers would see that I felt very unprepared. They had agreed to let me buy wholesale space for one issue. Then I began on foot to call on the local merchants. I sold them my "Window Wishing" column with my comments as a shopper. My advertisers paid full price. I paid the wholesale ad price. The difference was my profit. If I filled the column I earned twenty dollars a week and I could pay the eighty-dollar house payment. I never stopped until I reached that goal and more.

I had a wonderful treasure to help me with my fledging business: The Baldwin Park Library. Every evening I ran over and picked up books on advertising, business, and sales. I have always heard the voices in books. All the great minds waited for me there. I agree with Gilbert Highet, literary critic, who said: "Books are not lumps of lifeless paper, but minds alive on the shelves. From each goes out its own voice... just as the touch of a button can fill your room with music. By taking down a book and opening it, one can call into range the voice of a person far distant in time and space and hear that person speak to us, mind to mind, heart to heart." It was at the library that I met advertising genius Bruce Barton. I read all of his books, then read them again. One day as I dashed into the newspaper office to turn in my column copy, the publisher handed me a notice from the Advertising Association. There was to be a meeting in San Francisco. Bruce Barton was the speaker!

San Francisco seemed as far away from Los Angeles as the moon. It took a lot of thinking and planning to put the money together for a plane ticket and to arrange for baby-sitters. But I made it. I stuffed apples and a small package of crackers in my purse because I did not have money for meals. I did not stay overnight. I just came to hear my "friend of the mind," Mr. Barton.

He had white hair, a slight build, and told enchanting stories. He said he based his advertising business on two things:

First, a Bible verse, "Agree with your adversary early." Mr. Barton explained that your customer relaxes when you see their side of the situation. Then it is easy to show them that your product or service is what they need to get what they want. "Be the buyer's assistant," he said.

Second, he asked the audience if we remembered the third verse of "Mary Has a Little Lamb." Everyone knew the first verse, a few the second, but no one could say the third. He recited it for us:

"Why does the lamb love Mary so?"
The eager children cry.
"Because Mary loves the lamb, you know,"
The teacher did reply."

I remember that I jumped as he hit the lectern with a loud bang as he repeated that third line for emphasis. Then he said, "It is about time we quit trying to shear these sheep and start loving them a little bit!"

Mr. Barton meant we must be on the customers' side. Care for their interests, help them. Because of his ideas, I built my small advertising business into all of southern California. I hired and trained 285 employees who sold over four thousand continuous-contract advertising accounts. We had four offices. My customers brought me other customers. Mr. Barton's principles became the foundation of my business. Still are.

I remember he told the audience, "If you practice doing things for other people until it becomes so much a habit that you are unconscious of it, all the good forces of the universe line up behind you in whatever you undertake to do."

But on that day in San Francisco I was so young, uneducated, and yearning desperately for knowledge and help for my tiny start-up business. I waited until his speech was over. It took a long time for everyone to shake his hand and finally leave. Then I walked up to Mr. Barton thinking, "How can I tell him that he is my teacher?"

I only had a moment with him. I timidly reached out my hand. He took it in both of his. I looked into his kind eyes and said, "Mr. Barton, I am the one who *heard* you."

Bruce Barton replied, "You are the one I came for."

Amelia Earhart

Having always been an avid reader of biography, I was particularly interested in Charles Lindberg's autobiography. He told me in his book that as he flew low over the dark Atlantic with no instruments, he was not alone. He heard clearly the voices of the great minds of the past, encouraging him, guiding him, telling him, "Fly on!"

It was in the summer after high school graduation when I was seventeen that I met Amelia Earhart. I was working seven days a week at two jobs. My mother could not find work.

The only jobs they suggested for girls in high school in those days was nurse or school teacher. As I read about Amelia I was filled with electricity. She said that girls should have dreams too. That we should do the things our hearts and our talents led us to.

Several of my friends called one week to tell me they would soon leave for college. Suddenly it hit me. I would not be able to go to college. They would go on, and I would be left behind. At that very moment I held Amelia Earhart's autobiography in my hand. This is what she told me: "Some of us have great runways already built for us. If you have one, take off! If you do not have one, remember—it is your responsibility to grab a shovel. You must build the runway, not only for yourself, but for all those who will follow you."

Like a flash of lightning, I realized my responsibility to work at the thing I was good at. The next day I applied to the *Los Angeles Times* and got a job in advertising.

My Speaking Career

I began speaking to promote the small advertising business I had started when my husband's business was failing. My column ran in the rural weekly, the *Baldwin Park Bulletin*. My speaking topic was: "What Does Your Customer Want?" I billed myself as "Your Customer." By speaking free to the Kiwanis, Rotary, Lions Club, and Chambers of Commerce, I built my advertising business.

The merchants asked me to start my own advertising media, which I did. I continued to speak to promote it, city by city. Then one day a man at the back of the room came up to me and asked what I would charge to speak to the employees of his three big department stores. That is how the door of opportunity opened to my becoming a professional speaker. Speaking has led me to platforms and opportunities all over the world.

Charles Roth

Not long after I became a professional speaker, I was invited to speak in Denver, Colorado. I told my audience the story of the library and all the great voices I hear in the books. One of those voices was that of Charles Roth who wrote *Secrets of Closing Sales*. I told of the desperation and despair I felt as I was trying to sell a big advertising account. Then I picked up Charles Roth's book and heard his voice speaking to me. I used the sales techniques Charles Roth gave me at the library and closed the sale.

Suddenly, out in the audience a man stood up. He ran down the aisle, jumped up the stairs, dashed across the stage, and grabbed the mike out of my hand. I was astounded!

"I am Charles Roth!" he yelled. "You are the first woman speaker I have ever heard. I want you to know that I absolutely did write that book just for you, Dottie Walters. Don't you know that every author writes for the listening heart?" As we hugged there on stage, we were both crying.

There are some great women speakers from the Civil War period who made a tremendous difference in our country because of their speaking. If we could travel back in time, I would be so proud to have been in their audiences.

One of my favorite valiant women speakers was Harriet Tubman, who was born a slave. She escaped in 1849 through the Underground Railroad run by the Quakers. Harriet returned to help other slaves escape, which was particularly dangerous for her own safety. She made twenty round trips, until she had assisted over three hundred slaves to achieve freedom, including at last, her own mother and father. I love this quote which she used as she spoke on the platforms of her time: "When I found that I had crossed that line, I looked at my hands to see if I was the same person. There was such a glory over everything: the sun came like gold through the trees and over the fields, and I felt like I was in Heaven."

Another favorite of mine is a courageous white woman, Susan B. Anthony. She labored long and diligently to raise money to free the slaves and help the Underground Railroads. She served as an agent for the American Anti-Slavery Society.

However, at an abolitionist meeting, she raised her hand to be recognized. She and the other women present were told to move to the balcony, because as women, they had no right to speak.

They say there is "no fury like a woman scorned," especially so when she rightfully deserves respect and recognition. Susan arose, left the hall, and started the first International Council of Women and the National Woman Suffrage Alliance. It was due to her work that my mother was one of the first women to be allowed to vote in the United States. One of my favorite Susan B. Anthony quotes is this one: "Men, their rights and nothing more. Women, their rights and nothing less."

Another great woman who spoke on the Chautauqua circuit in those days was former slave Sojourner Truth. She lost her five children when they were sold away from her and gathered great support from all who heard her. In 1870 she spoke to members of Congress in an effort to persuade them to allot land to ex-slaves so that they could settle in the West. That speech was one of the greatest ever presented by any woman, at any time. Her life story embodied all the evils of slavery and all the hopes for the future.

In the following chapters, I will tell you about more of the greatest speakers I have ever heard, and of the speakers who inspired them to turn on the ignition and take off on their runways, or, to grab a shovel and build one.

Napoleon Hill

Author *Think and Grow Rich*. Shown here with
the typewriter he used to write that book.
Revered all over the world.

CHAPTER 4

Napoleon Hill

Little did I think, as I read the story of how the young newspaperman Napoleon Hill interviewed Andrew Carnegie, the steel magnate, that I would actually have the privilege of knowing Mr. Hill!

Andrew Carnegie's story fascinates me. His family left Scotland, where they were cottage weavers, because they were starving. Like most of our ancestors, they came to America for opportunity and freedom.

In America a kind man let boys come and read the books in his library. (When Andrew Carnegie grew up, he donated libraries to thousands of cities.) Young Andy read many books in this way. One of Andrew's neighbors was a telegrapher. He taught the eager boy the Morse Code, and let him replace him while he had his dinner. Then when President Abraham Lincoln put out a call for telegraph operators, Andrew was one of the first to apply. He ran the telegraph apparatus on the Civil War ammunition trains. It was when he noticed the frailty of the wooden bridges under the weight of the heavy war armaments, that Andrew began to think that steel would be the business to enter after the Civil War. He did so, becoming the greatest steel producer in the United States.

Andrew Carnegie surrounded himself with brilliant friends and employees. He liked a young newspaper reporter, Napoleon Hill (twenty-five years old), who was sent to interview him. Carnegie challenged Napoleon Hill to organize and interpret the American philosophy of personal achievement and write a book about it.

With Carnegie's help, Hill interviewed over five hundred successful American business people. Among them were Henry Ford, Tom Edison, and Alexander Graham Bell. From these personal interviews Napoleon Hill wrote his world-famous book, *Think and Grow Rich*. The title came to him in a dream. Over fourteen million copies have been sold and translated into seven languages.

I met Napoleon Hill because the publisher of my first book, *Never Underestimate the Selling Power of a Woman,* arranged for me to fly to New York to be interviewed on the top TV game show, "To Tell The Truth."

What an exciting experience! My publisher had sent a copy of my book to Napoleon Hill because it was the first book in the world written by a saleswoman for women in sales. You see, I visualized my book on the shelf of the little Baldwin Park Library long before it was published. I read *Think and Grow Rich* and knew Napoleon Hill was right: "Whatever the mind can conceive and believe, the mind can achieve."

I met many skeptics who told me, "Well Dottie, I don't believe you can accomplish what you have set out to do. Who do you think you are? After all 'seeing is believing.'"

I knew they were wrong; Napoleon Hill and Marcus Aurelius were right. The order is: Visualizing (conceiving), then believing, then persistent action. When dreams become reality, others see what you have seen all along.

The panel of celebrities on the nationwide show did not guess that I was the "real Dottie Walters" who wrote the book. One of the questions the panel of celebrities asked me and the two impostors was, "Who was the father of American advertising?" The other two women pretending to be me named well-known advertising men.

I answered, "Benjamin Franklin!" (Ben's cartoon of the snake cut apart with the legend, "If we don't hang together we will hang separately" was a powerful influence in uniting the American colonies.)

The panel chose a woman who sold undergarments for a New York department store. Then they had the "real Dottie Walters stand up!"

When we arrived back home in California, a letter awaited me. It was from Napoleon Hill. He said his wife did not guess me either. How could anyone believe that a plain, uneducated housewife from a rural chicken ranching town in California could be the author of the first book ever written by a saleswoman for women in sales and be the creator of a big advertising company? Impossible!

Napoleon Hill wrote to me about the things he was working on, his new projects. He closed with this question, "Dottie Walters, how does it feel to have blown a handful of stardust to the world?"

The brilliant businessman and speaker W. Clement Stone is president of the Napoleon Hill Foundation, which publishes the wonderful Napoleon Hill newsletter, *Think and Grow Rich*. I was honored when the publication recently featured my story on their front page and called it, "The Wonderful Letter."

Michael Ritt, executive director for the Napoleon Hill Foundation added this to the article. "Napoleon Hill wrote his letter to Dottie Walters on the same L. C. Smith, iron, non-electric typewriter he used to write *Think and Grow Rich*.

Napoleon Hill lived his philosophy. Aristotle was right. Thousands upon thousands of people have been inspired and helped by Napoleon Hill's book. I meet them as I speak in many countries.

Victor Kiam, a dynamic speaker, is the brilliant businessman who turned around the Remington Shaver business. He has on his office wall a plain wooden-framed parchment he found in a dusty corner of an antique shop: "If you must speak ill of another, do not say it, write it in the sand near the water's edge." —Napoleon Hill.

How W. Clement Stone met and became a business partner with Napoleon Hill after hearing Hill speak, is a fascinating story.

W. Clement Stone

One of the most exciting speakers I have ever heard is W. Clement Stone. My favorite story from his speech is about his selling newspapers at the age of six on the corner of 31st and Cottage Grove in Chicago. Mr. Stone went on to create Aon Corporation, a multi-million-dollar insurance empire. He is chairman of the board.

On that Chicago street, young Clement bought his papers at wholesale with borrowed money. All he had to do was to sell them to repay the loan and then make a

W. Clement Stone
President, Napoleon Hill Foundation, brilliant
businessman, author and speaker

profit, the vendor explained. Sounds simple. He picked up the papers and began his sales career, almost.

A group of bullies shoved and pushed the little boy and told him to get lost. It was their corner. Instead of running away, Clement turned around and saw a restaurant behind him. Through the big plate glass window he could see rows of business people eating breakfast. But he observed something else. (My friend of the mind Ben Franklin's most repeated phrase in all of his writing is, "I observed.") The breakfasters had no morning paper to enjoy with their meal! He ducked inside and began selling papers to those seated at the tables, delivering them with a big smile and a thank you. The owner of the restaurant ran him out! He had never allowed paperboys inside.

Clement didn't give up. He stood outside on the very edge of the plate glass window and watched. When the owner went into the kitchen, he dashed back in and sold more papers and got thrown out again. After several repetitions of this scene, the owner was furious. But the customers loved it. What spirit the boy had! They cheered him on and prevailed upon the owner to allow this bright, smiling, and persistent boy to bring his papers to them. He returned to the same restaurant every day and became good friends with the owner and his customers.

Later, when he joined his mother in the insurance business, he used the same technique. He sold insurance by going into stores and banks. He first sold the boss, then the employees. He made friends. Then he sold them more. He sold as many policies in a week as many did in months. His secret? He said he learned how to "recognize, relate, assimilate, and apply principles from one activity to another."

W. Clement Stone loved Napoleon Hill's book, *Think and Grow Rich*. He was determined to meet him. When he heard that Mr. Hill was the speaker at a service club luncheon in Chicago, Mr. Stone was there in the audience.

They became partners and co-authored *Success Through a Positive Mental Attitude*. Mr. Stone now administers the Positive Mental Attitude, PMA Foundation, perpetuating the lifetime research, writing, and teachings of Napoleon Hill.

Mr. and Mrs. Earl Nightingale

Earl was famous for worldwide radio shows.
He was an author, a speaker and the founder,
Nightingale Conant audio company

Mr. Stone was the publisher of *SUCCESS Magazine* as I began my business. The magazine published several of my articles and invited me to speak at their PMA rallies held in sports arenas. I appeared on many radio and TV shows promoting the big events for them.

My daughter Lilly and I are very proud that Mr. Scott DeGarmo, the present editor of *SUCCESS*, has reviewed several of our books and audio albums in their pages. We are delighted to be longtime friends of *SUCCESS* and to practice W. Clement Stone's solid ideas of repeat business through service, caring, and persistence!

"Lack of persistence is one of the major causes of failure. Create a definite plan for carrying out your desire. Begin at once whether you are ready or not to put this plan into action." —Napoleon Hill

Earl Nightingale

Napoleon Hill said to me, "Earl Nightingale, a local radio announcer, was 'shocked into the big money' by reading *Think and Grow Rich.*" What a magnificent link there is in those who throw open the gates of the genius river! Earl's radio shows are heard all over the world. The first time I became aware of Earl was when my husband had helped me to buy a very old model A Ford to use to run around town and pick up ad copy from my customers. The payments on that car seemed enormous to me.

I had an old portable battery-run radio I took with me in the car so that I would not miss listening to Earl Nightingale. His voice, so full of hope and positive ideas, seemed like a life preserver thrown to me as I struggled to stay afloat in a very choppy sea of difficulties.

My work system was to set up ad sales appointments on the phone. I paid a high school girl to stay with my children two hours after school while I buzzed out in my little Ford to pick up ad copy. One dark rainy day, the four ad customers whose ads I had counted on to make the house and car payment all turned me down. "Why?" I asked.

All four told me the same story. "Since the president of the Chamber of Commerce, Mr. Ahlman of the Rexall drugstore, does not buy your shoppers' column ads, the column must not be any good." I was stunned.

Then I remembered Earl Nightingale's words about the law of physics. "For every action there is an opposite and equal re-action."

If we need to change the re-action, we must go back to the causative action. Mr. Ahlman was always out, or too busy to speak to me. I decided to go immediately and try once more to talk to him. I parked my old car out in front, walked in, and I found him at the back of the small drugstore, filling prescriptions. My heart soared.

"I screwed my courage to the sticking place," as Will Shakespeare advised me, smiled confidently, and held up my shoppers' column in the *Baldwin Park Bulletin*. I told Mr. Ahlman how much the businesspeople in the community thought of his opinion. I asked him to please look at my work and give me something to tell them when they asked me what he thought of it.

If you have ever been hit hard in the stomach and had all of the air knocked out of you until you could barely stand up, you can imagine how I felt as Mr. Ahlman slowly turned his head from side to side in an emphatic, silent, "NO."

I staggered toward the front of the store thinking there was nowhere else to turn—I had lost our house and the car!

Toward the front of the drugstore was a beautiful old oak soda fountain. I sat down on the nearest stool, thinking I couldn't make it out to the car.

When the soda clerk walked up expectantly, I pulled the last dime out of my purse and ordered a cherry coke. The tears were very close to the surface as I tried to sip it, clutching my newspaper with my shoppers' column outlined in green crayon. (I had thought "green for GO!")

A lady with a very kind face sat next to me. She looked at me and asked what was wrong. Her tone was so sweet, I poured out my story about the four businesses who had turned me down that afternoon.

"If Mr. Ahlman would only look at my work!" I choked. "I'm going to lose our home. I don't know where to turn." I bit down hard on my lip, determined to hold back the tears of despair.

"Let me look at that newspaper column!" she said and took it right out of my hand. I wondered why she wanted to read it.

I remember that my coke was down to the bottom of the glass and the straw gurgled, when she suddenly spun the stool around and jumped down to the floor.

"Reuben Ahlman, you come right out here!" she yelled.

As he came running to the soda fountain she said to him, "Honey, you buy an ad from this girl." Then she turned back to me and said, "Give me the names of those four merchants. I'll go and phone them and you can go back and get their ads today." It was Mrs. Ahlman!

I had been talking to the wrong person.

The real story was that Mr. Ahlman was such a sweet man, he bought from everybody. He promised his wife that he would let her handle all of the advertising. Earl Nightingale was right. My action of insisting that I must sell Mr. Ahlman, without finding out how they ran their business, resulted in his negative re-action—"No."

As soon as I understood where my action should have been, my newspaper column filled up with ads. We became best friends with Mr. and Mrs. Ahlman. They arranged for the Chamber of Commerce to honor me with a "Dottie Walters' Banquet" a few years later.

My husband Bob bought the soda fountain when Mr. Ahlman took it out of his drugstore. Bob and our son Mike installed it here in my office. We serve visitors cherry cokes and lots of love. The famous self-esteem expert and great speaker Mr. Jack Canfield, wrote about my beautiful old soda fountain when he attended a seminar here at our ranch in Glendora, California. He used the story in his audio album for Nightingale-Conant.

I went to hear Earl Nightingale speak in person as often as he appeared in Los Angeles. I always loved best Earl's story of the law of physics. He stood quite still as he spoke, no matter how big the crowd. Then that magical deep voice lifted our minds up into the air as he told us stories and gave us hope and courage.

One of my favorite Nightingale quotes is this one, which helped me through some hard times and difficult people: "Arrogance is God's gift to shallow people." I often sent Earl articles and essays that I wrote about selling. What a thrill when he used them on his programs, always giving me credit. Earl particularly liked and used this story I wrote:

Ancient Chinese Secret

In the Chinese language whole words are written with a symbol. Often two completely unlike symbols, when put together, have a meaning different than either of their two separate components.

An example is the symbol for "man" and that for "woman." These two symbols standing together, mean "good."

The two symbols for "trouble" and "gathering crisis," when brought together, mean "opportunity."

As the answers always lie in the questions, so the opportunities of life lie directly in our problems. Thomas Edison said, "There is much more opportunity than there are people who can see it."

Great leaders emerge when a crisis occurs. In the life of people of achievement, we read repeatedly of terrible trouble which forced them to rise above the commonplace. In finding the answers, they discovered a tremendous power within themselves. Like a ground swell far out in the ocean, this force within explodes into a mighty wave when we overcome.

Then out steps the athlete, author, statesperson, scientist, the businessperson creating jobs for many people. David Sarnoff of RCA said, "There is plenty of security in the cemetery; I long only for opportunity."

People of achievement know this secret. The winds of adversity cannot shake them. Charles Lummis, first editor of the Los Angeles Times said, "I am bigger than anything that can happen to me. All these things,

sorrow, misfortune, and suffering, are outside my door.
I am in the house and I have the key!"

   Hidden in trouble hides the shining key, our
own magnificent opportunity.

I asked Earl to write the introduction for my first book, *Never Underestimate the Selling Power of a Woman.* Despite the fact that most businesspeople felt women should stay home "barefoot and pregnant," Earl responded immediately. Most recently I asked Earl to write the foreword to the book Lilly and I wrote together, *Speak & Grow Rich* (Prentice Hall). He and his lovely wife Diana invited me to come to Phoenix to visit with them and to pick up the foreword. Their gorgeous home was built in Navaho style. At the bottom level was Earl's big radio studio where he recorded all of his international radio programs.

Earl asked me if I would like to see where he wrote his scripts. Would I ever! We went up to the very top room, where the view was 180 degrees around the lovely Paradise Valley.

He told me he got the idea in the middle of the night for his best-selling audio product, "The Strangest Secret." This was the first talking record ever produced by the world famous Nightingale-Conant company, and is still a best seller.

The secret of Earl's "strangest secret" is the law of physics that saved my advertising business. Earl told me he got up, wrote the manuscript, and then recorded it as the sun came up, all in the same night. He said he loved to work on creative ideas in the very early morning, when the genius river flows without distraction.

There must be thousands of people around the world who hear Earl Nightingale's voice and his recorded audio albums. How many of us he has helped! It is my delight to do a three-minute inspirational radio show for the Business Radio Network of Colorado. I am heard on radio stations in one hundred cities across the United States every day. I receive lots of letters from people starting out in business, or struggling to keep on going. I always answer every one, as Earl Nightingale did.

I wrote this little poem for my dear friend Earl Nightingale, who let the genius river flow through him.

The Genius River

Some say Genius is a person.
But the Ancients state "Not so.

Genius is a river's mighty flow.

There is more of it behind its dam
than ever flows before.

The channel's always gushing, pouring more."

To open Genius' floodgates, fill your mind
with dreams.

Bar the door to "no," and "how it seems."

Allow your thoughts to wander; search for signs of
what can be!

Then plan and work, and use your industry.

For the Genius River's rising; heartbeat close it
pounds—at hand!

Like the Genie of the lamp who shouts:
"Command!"

Chapter 5

Jack Swartz

Nowadays, many speakers specialize in teaching telephone technique. The phone is a tool every business uses. It was my privilege to hear and be advised by one of the first great speakers on the subject. Jack Swartz wrote a best-selling book about telephone sales and gave me lots of ideas for my own speaking career. He was a kind and generous man.

His unique idea for programs was that the company he spoke for set up an outside phone line right on the stage. Jack took the actual list of the client's customers and called them during his program. Both sides of the conversations were broadcast to the audience. I remember thinking what a risk he took!

After three rings he yelled at the audience, "Hang Up! They aren't there! Don't waste your time—punch in another number and increase your odds!" During his hour and a half presentation, he made five live telephone calls, interspersed with excellent telephone technique advice.

If the party did not answer, Jack said, "That's okay! I know that every time I punch in a number I've earned money, because I know the odds of the calls I make to the sales I close. I make money every time I pick up the phone and call a number. And so can you!"

He closed his program with a live phone call to a man who was completely paralyzed, but who made his living through telephone sales. He used his tongue to dial numbers and a recording machine to make a record of the sale.

There were tears in everyone's eyes as this brave man told the audience via phone line what it meant to him to be able to support his family by using Jack Swartz's telephone sales techniques. Jack was a magnificent showman.

Elmer Wheeler

Another famous author/speaker who inspired and helped me was Elmer Wheeler. Elmer's exciting book *Selling the Sizzle* was a smash hit. The title means "sell benefits, benefits, benefits." Elmer was booked by big companies to figure out "sizzle words" their sales people could use to increase sales.

The Wheeler story I remember and love best was about Walgreen's drugstores. Their soda fountain business had fallen off in all of their chain of stores across the United States. Elmer was called in to figure out what to do. He spent a lot of time sitting on those drugstore stools listening and learning.

This is what he came up with: He had the Walgreen's waiter or waitress say to each customer who ordered a malted milk: "Eggs make your skin and hair beautiful naturally! Would you prefer one egg or two with your malted milk?" (Note, they did NOT say, "Do you want any eggs?")

The results of the words in the first sentence and the choice of two positives in the second sentence were astonishing! Those hot words not only increased each of Walgreen's drugstore fountain sales several hundred percent, they gave a great boost to the egg industry, the trucking industry, and the feed business. Sales make the wheels of industry hum. This was Elmer Wheeler's famous "Sizzle System."

He told another story about when he first began speaking. In those depression days people bought just one or two gallons of gas at a time. One of the big oil companies booked him to find sizzle words to increase gas station sales. Elmer had their employees smile and say, "Hello! Thanks for coming in today. Fill 'er up?" The positive suggestion made all the difference. Still does.

He was a wonderful man who walked his talk. My favorite quote by Elmer Wheeler is: "The real wit tells jokes to make others feel superior, while the half-wit tells them to make others feel small."

Zig Ziglar

I first heard Zig Ziglar with his great exuberant talent when I spoke on the same platform with him for the Salesmasters group. Zig uses "down home" stories from his own Yazoo City, Mississippi, life. He says he speaks in a fast style of about 220 words a minute with "gusts of up to 550."

Zig used a big metal farm kitchen pump as a prop to illustrate his story of the need to put water into the pump in order to prime it. It won't work until YOU do.

Zig said if we don't put something into life, we will never get anything out. He called his program, "Biscuits, Pump Handles & Fleas." The first edition of his book had the same name; then his new publisher changed it to, *See You at the Top*. I love Zig's description of himself: "I fit people with new glasses—not rose-colored, but magnifying glasses."

Zig had a very hard childhood. His wonderful mother was widowed and worked under great difficulties to raise her children alone. Maybe that was why he was taken aback by my being on the same program that day. His ideal was to have women stay home. However, God gave us all different sets of talents and circumstances. My experience is that "one size fits all" in anything is one "lollapaloosa" of a lie (My family begs me not to cook!).

I learned many good things by watching Zig. He moves around the stage because he believes an audience pays attention for only a few minutes.

He goes out into the audience before the program and at intermission to talk to people one to one. His fans follow him wherever he speaks to hear him again and again, because he speaks to them individually about their dreams and hopes. He truly loves each one. They know it.

Zig began his career in the aluminum pot and pan sales business, as did his brother Judge Ziglar. What a magnificent business and life work he has accomplished. He is a very devout and active Baptist, who lives his religion in everything he does.

Zig Ziglar
Sales speaker, author of *See You at the Top*

John Goddard

All four of the children we have had the privilege of raising here on our ranch experienced this great speaker during their high school years. John Goddard is a real life "Indiana Jones" who set out to accomplish a startling list of goals in his life. His subject—"Goal Setting: The High Road to Adventurous Living."

When John was fifteen he made a list of 127 challenging lifetime goals. To date he has achieved well over one hundred of them. He led the first expedition to explore the length of the Nile, the world's longest river, by kayak. He became the first man to explore from source to mouth the second largest river, the Congo (Zaire).

John has set records as a civilian jet flier. His anthropological studies of 260 tribal societies in all parts of the globe are fascinating and most valuable to science.

No wonder my children and I were so moved by this great man who is a fellow of the Royal Geographical Society and the Explorer's Club. John Goddard was inspired by Dr. Rufus B. von Kleinsmid, president of the University of Southern California.

John explained to me, "The most cherished memory I have of him was when, as an entering freshman, I attended his welcoming speech in Bovard Auditorium on the USC campus.

"Dr. von Kleinsmid told us, 'The effort of becoming a truly educated person is not a finite goal, but a never-ending, life-long process of ever-increasing wisdom and appreciation of life, and a greater tolerance for others, especially those who are different in race or religion.'"

Most recently John Goddard flew the computerized plane used extensively in the Gulf War, the F-15 Eagle, at nine hundred miles per hour. The slightest touch to the steering mechanism sends this plane zooming off in a new direction before a correction can be made.

I hope your children have been privileged to hear the great speaker John Goddard or that you have heard him speak in business meetings. Perhaps you have read of him in *Time* and *Newsweek* magazines when they recently published the news of his receiving the Encyclopaedia

John Goddard
Modern "Indiana Jones," world's greatest
goal setter

Britannica "Achievement in Life" Award. No one is ever the same again after hearing him.

John Goddard's greatest achievement of all, in my mind, is his inspirational message to thousands and thousands of children to become all they can be. The parents of America thank you, John Goddard.

Bob Richards

Dynamic Bob Richards was a member of three Olympic teams, the only pole vaulter in Olympic history to win the Gold Medal twice. The sportswriters voted him to the All-Time Olympic Team. Bob was a broadcaster for CBS and NBC. He has seven Hall of Fame Awards.

Bob Richards has inspired audiences all over the world. As a little girl I remember seeing his picture on the boxes of our breakfast Wheaties, the "Breakfast of Champions!"

I asked Bob to tell us about the great speakers who inspired him. Bob said there were two. First, Jesse Owens, the Olympic winner of 1936, who was called the "world's fastest human." Jesse won four gold medals in Berlin, Germany.

Black Jesse Owens triumphed in the broad jump against white Luz Long, Adolph Hitler's own Aryan champion. Adolf Hitler was humiliated. He made the two men repeat the event, saying that Owens had overstepped the mark. Owens moved far back of the mark—and won again. He conclusively shattered Hitler's claims of "Aryan superiority" in front of the whole world. (Jesse became best friends with Luz Long, which says a lot about both men.)

Owens became a tremendous speaker who inspired both youth and adults. Here is the Jesse Owens quote Bob Richards remembers best:

"You see, black isn't beautiful;
White isn't beautiful.
Skin-deep is never beautiful.
Human beings come in colors
like circles in the Olympic flag, linked in love.
That is beautiful."

Bob Richards
Olympic Decathlon champion, speaker/writer

The first time I heard Bob Richards speak, I remember the story he told of being in the audience of Peter Marshall, chaplain to the United States Senate. Some of Bob's friends wanted to go and hear Peter Marshall speak at a church, but Bob didn't want to go. He finally accompanied his friends and was thrilled with the great voice and marvelous stories Peter Marshall told.

Bob tells the story about Peter describing a street scene in the Holy Land—the heat, dust, insects, animals, palm trees, and blazing desert sun. As Peter spoke, the walls of the auditorium fell away! Bob said he saw the peddlers and their heavy loads, wagons full of merchandise, heard the buzz of flies.

Along the side of the dusty street was a pale woman who seemed about to die. She could barely move. But her eyes were full of hope because she was waiting for Jesus and his disciples to come by. She had faith that He would heal her of her never-ending hemorrhage.

Just then, Bob said he heard angry shouts and pounding hooves. The audience actually turned their heads to see the Roman chariots race madly by, scattering everyone in their path!

The woman was knocked roughly to one side. She got up again, slowly, painfully, and looked with longing eyes down the road. Bob said that by this time everyone was sitting on the edge of their chairs. The audience urged the woman on! All of this scene was projected by Peter Marshall onto the screen of their minds.

At last Jesus and the disciples came down the road, but they almost passed her by. Peter Marshall's voice raised in a crescendo, the crowd was hushed, holding their breath.

With one last tremendous effort the woman lurched forward—Peter Marshall stopped. Paused. Then he held the microphone close to his mouth and whispered, "and then, she touched Him!"

There was not a dry eye in the auditorium. Peter Marshall's story changed Bob Richards' life forever that day.

Bob Richards, the tremendous Olympian, now changes lives for good, every time he speaks.

Chin-Ning Chu
Chinese-American speaker, consultant, author
on ancient *Chinese Book of War*

Chin-Ning Chu

Chin-Ning Chu is not only a talented writer (*The Chinese Mind Game, The Asian Mind Game, and Thick Face, Black Heart*), she is considered the foremost expert in the world on Asian wisdom, business psyche, and strategic winning tactics. You may have seen her on many TV shows such as "Larry King Live," "Sonya Live" and many more national programs.

As I listen to Chin-Ning speak, I am so impressed with her knowledge and determined, vibrant personality. She is often invited to comment on the current affairs of Asia by network television and national radio stations.

What a fascinating speaker! Chin-Ning was born in China to a wealthy Manchurian landlord family. At the age of three, Chin-Ning and her family fled from the Communists in Tianjim, traveling to Shanghai and later to Taiwan for safety.

While in college, Chin-Ning managed a full course load while handling the marketing responsibilities of a pharmaceutical company and two other firms. Her programs and books are based on ancient oriental books of strategy and wisdom, which make her material unique and completely fascinating.

Chin-Ning often quotes Swami Muktananda (Baba) who said:

"In praise or blame, honor or insult,
keep your mind still.

Remain the same in solitude or among throngs.

Even in your dreams, never be down cast.

Everything exists in the imagination alone."

When I asked Chin-Ning which speaker personally inspired her, she said, "It is Gurumayi Chidvilasananda. I would travel thousands of miles to hear her profound wisdom. Her words are immortal. They pierce the listener's heart. Her description of listening to her teacher, Swami Muktananda, is so beautiful. It communicates the same

Harvey Mackay
Chairman and CEO, Mackay Envelope
Corporation, author/speaker/
entrepreneur/businessman

sentiment I experience when I hear her. Here are her thoughts. They describe how her words have touched me.

"Gurumayi Chidvilasananda said, 'I used to wonder at the power of Baba's (Swami Muktananda) words. No matter how simple they appeared to be, they were immensely potent. It was not that I loved him: the mere sound of his words bewitched me. Every word he uttered would resonate throughout my being and completely permeate me, and would invariably trigger in me new understanding. For years I wondered why his word carried so much force. Then one day I realized that it was because he was established in Truth. Therefore, his words function as mantras (sacred words invested with the power to transform and protect the individual who repeats them).'"

Chin-Ning credits Gurumayi's words with "transforming me, an ordinary Chinese girl, into an English language author and international speaker. Through these teachings I learned how to tap into the Way of Natural Knowing; the source of all knowledge."

I would disagree with my friend, the great speaker Chin-Ning, only with the use of the word "ordinary" in describing herself.

Harvey Mackay

I like many things about Harvey Mackay. His delivery on the platform is powerful but sincere. He has an honest, bright, feel about him. If I were to pick someone who personifies American free enterprise, I would choose him. Harvey is what we in the speakers bureau business hear our meeting-planner clients call "a real person," because he talks about what he knows about. He has been there, he has done it. All of his creative ideas are based on practical, sturdy, and workable frameworks.

Harvey tells the story of surrounding himself with wise people when he bought his envelope company at age twenty-five. Harvey was smart enough to ask the "old-timers" in the company for advice and help. He believes in asking for advice, support, and help.

He is a mentor to thousands of businesses through his speeches; his books: *Swim with the Sharks Without Being*

Eaten Alive—named the number one business book in America for 1988—and *Beware the Naked Man Who Offers You His Shirt*, Mackay's second *New York Times* number one bestseller, and *Sharkproof* (which has just been released); and his other unique products, plus, through his excellent syndicated business column, "Strictly Business," he continues to appreciate and profit from the wisdom of others.

Harvey tells the story of his first business mentor, his father-in-law, who was a self-educated man without a high school diploma. Harvey says, "He knew the value of one human being. He believed that one person can make a difference."

My personal favorite of Harvey's quotes is: "The best way to be a winner is to surround yourself with winners."

I remember Andrew Carnegie saying the very same thing. We asked Harvey which quote he loves most of all. He replied: "Walk your company floor every day of every week of every year. Catch one of your people doing something right, and then in front of Mother, God, and Country, praise them." —Ken Blanchard.

Who was the great speaker who turned American businessman Harvey Mackay on? Harvey told me: "Dottie, without a doubt the greatest speaker I've ever heard was Dr. Norman Vincent Peale. Whether he talked to a two-person lemonade stand, or twenty thousand veterans of foreign wars, his concentrated focus made you feel he was talking only to you.

"As Dr. Peale spoke, your heart and mind pumped with the awesome adrenaline power of positive thought. I first heard him over twenty-five years ago and I can honestly say, he never missed a beat in a quarter-century. He literally lifted the human spirit of millions the world over. In my book, Dr. Norman Vincent Peale should be declared an international treasure."

Harvey is chairman of the board and CEO of Mackay Envelope Corporation, which employs four hundred people and manufactures over ten million envelopes per day. The list of the organizations where he has served as president, such as the Young President's Organization, Twin Cities Chapter, is a very long list. He has received many honors including one from Toastmaster's International as "one of the five top speakers in the world."

In our next chapter you will meet some of the most fascinating and unusual speakers in the world!

Bishop Fulton J. Sheen

One of the most beloved American speakers
by all faiths

Credit: Sheen Productions, Inc., New York

Chapter 6

Bishop Fulton J. Sheen

I hope you remember, as I do, how a few years ago we eagerly awaited the weekly television shows presented by master speaker Bishop Sheen. He did not stand still as he spoke. His every movement had power. His Bishop's robes flowed gracefully as he spoke to the camera and right to the heart of every listener.

When he looked directly at us his penetrating eyes grabbed our attention and never let us go. He seemed to beam a power force of love right through our television screen.

Bishop Sheen was a consummate storyteller. He talked about human foibles, hopes, and dreams of those from biblical times to the present—tales of courage about people who got up again when they were knocked down. A remarkable man. His stories sliced across all religions and creeds in an ecumenical style that reached us all. Switching from every other TV channel when his program aired, everyone loved him and tuned in to hear him.

Bishop Sheen never ranted, raved, yelled, or pounded the lectern. He enchanted us with eloquent stories that he painted on the canvas of our minds, accenting his warm voice with tones of bright humor as well as dark pathos. His voice was loud, then soft, inspiring and urging us to "press on to our own higher potential," as Paul of Tarsus did.

He advised, "Live each day as you would climb a mountain. An occasional glance toward the summit keeps the goal in mind, but many beautiful scenes are to be observed from each new vantage point. So climb slowly, enjoying each passing moment; and the view from the summit will serve a more rewarding climax for your journey."

One of my favorite Bishop Sheen stories was a tale about his being scheduled to speak in Philadelphia at the Town Hall. It was a lovely evening so he decided to leave

Michael Geraghty
Charming Irish-American expert on negotiation
with Oriental business people

early and walk from the hotel to the auditorium. However, because he was a stranger in town, he took a wrong turn and then another, until finally he realized he was hopelessly lost.

Seeing a group of teenagers on the sidewalk, Bishop Sheen asked for directions. They looked him up and down and asked him why he was going to the Town Hall.

"I'm going to give a speech," the Bishop replied.

"About what?" the kids asked.

"I will speak to the audience about how to get to heaven. Would you like to come along?"

Bishop Sheen then grinned at the camera and said the kids told him, "Are you kidding? You don't even know the way to Town Hall!"

Michael F. Geraghty

Another Catholic who reminds me of Bishop Sheen in his power, charm, and love for humankind is the great speaker Michael F. Geraghty. Michael has a marvelous, genuine Irish lilt to his speech. When he calls, he charms our speakers bureau office staff completely with his Irish sayings and wit.

Michael has led a most unusual life. Born in Ireland, he was trained and then ordained a Catholic priest. He is a brilliant man, a teacher, and a scholar in Greek and Latin.

Like many others—perhaps a few years ahead of changes by the church itself—Michael left the priesthood and married a lovely young woman. They are the parents of two beautiful daughters. He has an aura of uncritical, heartfelt caring for everyone in his life, which I saw also in Bishop Sheen.

My Scottish grandfather once said, "You could trust a man like that as a child trusts its parent, by crawling up onto the parent's lap, laying its head on the parent's shoulder, and going to sleep in perfect confidence."

Michael Geraghty is now a negotiation expert who is often sent to Japan where he handles contracts for American companies. I love Michael's story that most Americans want to get the bargain made quickly—the Ross Perot "fix-that-fast-and-MOVE-ON!" method.

However, Michael explains, the Japanese prefer to look upon negotiation as a farmer looks at the planting of a field. They desire crops for many years in the future.

When I asked Michael to tell me about the speakers who most inspired him, he said, "In June of 1969 I heard President John F. Kennedy speak in Galway City, Ireland. He was polished, excellent, and appealed to the head.

"However the most impressive speaker I ever heard was Karol Wotjyla, better known as John Paul II. He was spectacular and appealed to the heart. Coincidentally, the place again was Galway, Ireland, in October of 1979.

"The audience consisted of over a quarter-million young Irish people. The Pope spoke for thirty minutes. One sentence he used that memorable day I will take to my grave. He said quite unexpectedly, 'Young people of Ireland, I love you.'"

There was a moment of stunned silence. After all, popes are not supposed to say such things! Then the spontaneous ovation began, like a great tidal wave overwhelming everything in its roll.

It went on and on and on, for a full eight minutes. The Pope just stood there smiling at a quarter million young people who spontaneously started to sing to him.

Hardened television reporters couldn't believe what they were witnessing. The Pope later called the eight-minute ovation "a charismatic moment."

Michael says, "While I disagree strongly with some of his opinions, Karol Wotjyla is a fascinating human being, who happens to be Pope. The first non-Italian Pope in four centuries, he is the Pope who skis, writes plays, sings with Italian audiences, carries on a fascinating correspondence with Mikhail Gorbachev, and is an accomplished philosopher in his own right. Behind all his external charm lies Polish granite. That one charismatic moment in Galway City in 1969 captures the essence of a super communicator. He has the ability to relate to a huge audience and say, in one sentence, what will not only be remembered many years later, but handed on generation to generation by each of us who heard it."

When I asked Michael Geraghty to tell me the great quote he has remembered and lived by all of his life, he replied, "This was spoken by Patrick Brosnan, the wisest man I know. He is an old fisherman, Irish speaker, and friend, still young in his nineties, from Dingle, County Kerry, Ireland. I often think of him."

"If you lose your wealth, you have lost nothing.

If you lose your health, you have lost something.

But if you lose your integrity, everything is lost."

Bobbe L. Sommer, Ph.D.

Bobbe L. Sommer is one of the finest women speakers on the platform today.

She was inspired by Dr. Maxwell Maltz, a plastic surgeon who realized with shock and dismay that many of his patients believed that changing the shape of their face, nose, ears, or other body parts would solve all of their problems. They blamed everything that went wrong in their lives on their physical appearance. However, after the surgery, when they realized they were still the same person on the inside, and that it was the inside that people reacted to, they were devastated.

Dr. Maltz wrote a magnificent book which sold over thirty million copies titled, *Psycho-Cybernetics* (Prentice Hall). He spoke to thousands of audiences about the projected image of the insides of their heads, how to change it with good self-esteem, and how to set life goals.

It was in the early 1970s that Bobbe Sommer attended a program presented by Dr. Maxwell Maltz. That was a magic day.

It reminds me of one of my favorite stories about the *Lady of Shalott* by Alfred Lord Tennyson. The Lady was imprisoned in a tower, chained to a loom. As she worked day after day, she could see in a dark mirror hung on the wall above the loom the dim reflection of a window which revealed the road and the river below the tower. She could hear and dimly see the world and life go by, leaving her behind. She made no effort to escape.

Then one day she saw Sir Lancelot ride by in his shining armor with brilliant banners flying. Suddenly she stood erect, broke her chain with superhuman force, smashed the mirror, and broke the loom. She ran to the door,

Bobbe Sommer
Author/speaker, *Psycho-Cybernetics 2000*

flung it open, and escaped the tower. The Lady of Shalott found a boat, climbed in, and set sail for Camelot!

I can hear our friend of the mind Amelia Earhart saying, "Women need to do things too."

On the dramatic day that Bobbe attended Dr. Maltz' Psycho-Cybernetics program, he asked for volunteers from his large audience to demonstrate a point. Bobbe stood and raised her hand.

He chose her from all the volunteers to come up on stage. Then he asked her to claim a specific goal. One that would "make her heart sing!"

The answer was difficult for Bobbe. However, Dr. Maltz would not let her go. He kept quizzing her on stage until she reached down into her heart and told him and the audience a goal that would fit his specifications.

She said her heart's song was to be a professional speaker. She wanted to bring the message of the importance of self-esteem and "making the most of your best" to as many people as possible.

Maxwell Maltz ignited the fire of action for her when he flung high these banner words on the platform: "Somebody out there in the world is going to get your goals, so why not you?"

Bobbe left that auditorium and earned her Ph.D. in psychology. Then step by step and audience by audience, she became an internationally recognized authority on self-esteem and interpersonal communication.

She is a core trainer for Fortune 100 companies and major agencies of the U.S. government. She has written two books and created several audiotape series.

Next Bobbe decided to rewrite Dr. Maxwell Maltz's famous *Psycho-Cybernetics* book into a modern version titled *Psycho-Cybernetics 2000*, published by Prentice Hall. Bobbe included ideas for a new generation on the fundamentals of self-image, self-realization, biofeedback, positive self-talk, and image exercises in psychological improvement. This new book was an immediate bestseller, with 215,000 copies presold before it came off the press.

In speaking to her audiences, Bobbe often says, "Life is not about fairness. It is about choices."

Les Brown
"Mr. Inspiration," Dynamic speaker/author.
Recipient, Toastmasters' Golden Gavel Award

My own favorite quotes from Dr. Maltz are: "We must bet on our ideas, take the calculated risk, and ACT. Everyday living requires courage, if life is to be effective and bring happiness."

Les Brown

Les Brown is a remarkable man and a charismatic speaker. I was enchanted when I heard him speak, and was especially impressed with his own personal story. He began life with the greatest possible rejection. His birth mother became pregnant by another man while her husband was overseas in the military service. She gave Les and his fraternal twin brother up for adoption.

Les was adopted by a woman who has a great spirit. She raised the two boys all alone and became his magnificent inspiration.

However, for years Les hated his birth parents. He says it was a lot of work to hold that grudge. He finally dropped the heavy load of hate with the help of a quote from Kahlil Gibran: "Our children come through us, not from us."

Les says he realized that we are responsible for what we become. His adopted mama, Mrs. Mamie Brown, chose him by love.

Les explains that he has forgiven his birth parents. He plays with the hand life has dealt him and will not allow himself to be burdened with anger, resentment, regret, and guilt.

Another favorite speaker friend, Dr. Daniel Amen (author of *Don't Shoot Yourself in the Foot),* says the hardest person to change is one who continues to blame others.

I love Les Brown's words, "It is the person you become, not the things you achieve, that is most important."

Les says the source of his own determination is his mama's tremendous strength. She was left motherless as a baby. Her father was a migrant Florida crop picker. When she adopted the twin boys she had no immediate plan of action, but knew within her heart she could do it. She was willing to take a risk. Les dedicated his wonderful book, *Live Your Dreams* (Wm. Morrow & Co.), to his mama with this quote by Abraham Lincoln: "All

Don Hutson
Past president, National Speakers Association,
brilliant author/speaker

that I am, and all that I ever hope to be, I owe to my angel mother." (The lady was President Lincoln's step-mother.)

Mr. Leroy Washington, a high school drama coach, recognized the wonderful talent within Les, even though other teachers mistakenly labeled him "educable mentally retarded." Mr. Washington taught him that while we are not always able to control what life puts in our path, we can always control who we are and what we will become.

Les Brown served three terms in the Ohio State Legislature and is a very popular professional speaker, voted by Toastmasters International as one of the world's five best speakers for 1992. Les says, "My mission is to get a message out that will help people become uncomfortable with their mediocrity. A lot of people are content with their discontent. I want to enable them to see themselves having more, and achieving more."

One of Les Brown's favorite quotes is mine too, from George Bernard Shaw: "This is the true joy in life; the being used for a purpose recognized by yourself as a mighty one, the being thoroughly worn out before you are thrown on the scrap heap, the being a force of nature instead of a feverish, selfish little clod of ailments and grievances complaining that the world will not devote itself to making you happy."

Don Hutson

When the National Speakers Association was formed, I had been speaking for several years and eagerly joined as one of the first members. There were only a handful of women in that vanguard group. It was there I met and heard Don Hutson speak. He later served as their president. Don is the epitome of the prepared speaker. When I arranged for him to speak to the association of speakers bureaus, the International Group of Agencies & Bureaus, IGAB, which I founded, he interviewed every member and based his program on their needs. He made a profound impression.

I am particularly impressed with Don's emphasis on goal-setting. He tells his audience: "The more seriously a person takes the goal-setting process, the more likely he

Joel Goodman
CEO Humor Project. Author/speaker
about all things humorous

or she is to achieve great things. Success must be achieved principally by an energized vision of higher personal accomplishment. As soon as we put our visions and goals in writing, we have not only tripled our commitment, but also simultaneously tripled the probability of achieving them." Don certainly has inspired me to set and achieve goals.

When I asked Don which speaker had inspired him he told me this story. "The first time I heard my mentor, Dr. Kenneth McFarland, I was a senior in college and an impressionable twenty-year-old. His talk was so memorable and made such an impression that I went up to Dick Gardner, who was president of NSAE, which staged the event.

"I said I wanted to go to work for his company. I wanted to get closer to the power of the platform and the philosophies of Dr. McFarland and the other speakers that day.

"Ken McFarland, in my opinion, was well-tagged as the 'dean of American speakers.' His delivery, his pure eloquence, as well as his content, so activated me that I knew at that moment I had to hear more.

"We developed a wonderful friendship. After a few years when I was president of the National Speakers Association, he joined NSA and subsequently made a few talks for that group. I can truly say today that because of Ken McFarland, I am a better speaker, better American, a better Christian, and a better professional. God rest his great soul."

Dr. Joel Goodman

One of the qualities I see repeated in the life of every great speaker is the ability to concentrate on one thing until the speaker becomes a world expert on that subject. Sometimes the person whose heart is called to be a speaker is part of a huge audience, or sometimes one of an extremely small one.

This is the story of a humorist extraodinaire, Dr. Joel Goodman, who was part of a group of just two people when a talented speaker "turned on his ignition switch."

Alvin, a van driver, is the speaker who inspired Joel's amazing career. In 1976, Joel was a college professor who flew to Houston because his father faced surgery for a life-threatening aneurysm. Alvin drove Joel and his mother from the hotel to the hospital, all the while telling jokes and doing magic tricks.

"Mom and I were rigid with fear," Joel says. "Alvin transformed two stressed-out people into human beings who could laugh and chuckle. We let go of some of our terrible tension."

After his Dad recovered, Joel wondered, "Do we have to wait for the Alvins of the world to come along at the perfect moment, or can we be intentional about humor?"

Thus the "Joel Goodman Humor Project" was born. It is a clearinghouse for humor research. Joel himself is now a world class speaker on the subject of the power of humor. He has personally spoken to 500,000 people and answers 50,000 letters a year. The Humor Project's first conference in 1968 drew 450 people. Today thousands attend his twice-yearly conferences, which feature famous humorists such as Sid Caesar, Jay Leno, Victor Borge, and Steve Allen. Steve began his program for their convention with "I have known Shirley MacLain since she was a cocker spaniel!" Humorists attend from not only all fifty states, but Canada, Japan, Russia, Saudi Arabia, Sweden, Norway, England, Italy, Singapore, and South Africa.

Today, Joel Goodman's humor product catalog and conferences reach over a half-million people annually. Joel also publishes a magazine, *Laughing Matters,* which has subscribers in all fifty American states and in twenty other countries. Joel Goodman, "The Gigglemeister" passes out about 175 "humor grants" of money each year to spread good cheer in hospitals, schools, libraries, drug treatment centers, and prisons.

Joel is inspired by all humorists, especially Mark Twain, who said: "The old man laughed loud and joyously, shook up the details of his anatomy from head to foot, and ended by saying such a laugh was money in a man's pocket, because it cut down the doctor's bills like anything."

Joel often speaks at his "Staff Laff" programs with a nickel coin stuck to his forehead. He asks everyone in the audience to follow suit. "Why should we be serious about humor?" he asks. "There are three good reasons to use humor in our daily life: One, humor is a natural way of healing the body; two, it's a great way for handling stress and preventing burnout; three, we use humor to build and maintain relationships."

My favorite Joel Goodman quote, "He who laughs, lasts!"

In our next chapter, I will tell you a story that will amaze you. If it were the plot of a movie you would say, "No way—never!" But every word is true! Come with me and meet an astonishing great speaker whose name is most appropriate, "Eagles!"

Gil Eagles
Exciting mentalist, speaker, author, entertainer

Chapter 7

Gil Eagles: A Magic Story

This is a most unusual, magical story about Gil Eagles. Off stage, it has been my privilege to work with Gil Eagles' lovely wife, Esther, CEO of Eagles Talent Associates. She is my honored colleague in the speakers bureau world. Their brilliant teenage son is already presenting big shows featuring famous athletes for collectors of baseball cards. A completely creative family.

The first time I heard Gil Eagles speak I was enchanted, as was the rest of the audience. He is a dazzling mentalist, master hypnotist, and entertainer, who holds your attention in the palm of his hand. Gil is suave and sophisticated. He speaks eloquently and is a smooth showman with delightful timing. You may have seen him perform at Las Vegas, Atlantic City, or at any one of thousands of conventions.

It was his personal story which transfixed his audience! He was raised in Tanganyika, East Africa. His family spoke Polish and Yiddish in their home. Playing with his childhood friends he learned to speak fluent Swahili.

The family dreamed of moving to the United States. In preparation, they sent Gil away to an English boarding school. However, the change in mental climate from his loving family to an atmosphere where no one spoke any language he could understand, crashed the little boy into mental shock. He slammed the door of his mind on his teachers. They were unable to get through to him to teach him to read or write. He stuttered the few English words he had to learn in order to get along. Gil could not speak one single complete sentence.

The teachers finally concluded that he was not capable of learning more, so they assigned tasks to him which he could do with his hands. By the time his family was ready to set off for America, he had less than a grade school education and had never attended high school.

In America Gil got a job as busboy in a pizza restaurant on the New York beach boardwalk. By this time he was a twenty-one-year-old illiterate—in any language.

Magic occurred when a pizza customer left a tiny promotional phonograph record on the seat of one of the restaurant booths. The people who left it never returned, so Gil took it home. The miraculous thing is that if they had left a book, he could not have read it. The only way he could be reached was through audio. The title of the record was "Personal Motivation" by Paul J. Meyer of SMI, Waco, Texas. Paul Meyer began as a stutterer too. Gil played that little record on his sister's record player over and over again. Gil had never before heard of goal setting, positive thinking, or visualization.

As he listened to Paul Meyer speak, the sleeping giant of his brilliant mind awoke! Gil said, "I suddenly realized this record was made for me! I thought, I don't want to be like I am any more. I want to change."

His mind was like Dorothy's red shoes in the *Wizard of Oz*. He suddenly realized his intelligence had been there all the time, waiting to be used. Gil took his small busboy earnings and found a bookstore. "I want beginning books that will teach me to read and write," he stuttered. He taught himself.

Imagine emerging from the role of an illiterate busboy into a world famous speaker who receives many letters like this one, from Douglas L. Raymond, director of the "Ideas Workshop" of *Advertising Age Magazine*. "Gil Eagles' ability to communicate with our audience of professional communicators is amazing. Incredible!"

Gil told me, "Dottie, there were many wonderful things on that record, but the one that stands out most in my mind is this: 'That which we vividly imagine, sincerely desire, and ardently pursue, will inevitably come to pass.'

"There's an old maxim that says, 'When the student is ready, the guru will appear.'" Gil explained, "What made me ready was an internal realization that I was worthy and deserving of feeling good physically, emotionally, and mentally. I suddenly knew I was just like everyone else in the world. I realized my very existence and birthright entitled me to feel good, and most important of all, that I am the guy who is responsible for doing that which brings about my own good feelings.

"One of the first books I ever read was *As a Man Thinketh* by James Allen ("as a man thinketh, so is he" from the Bible). This book helped me strengthen my belief in the power of my mind and visualization. I heard the voice of Og Mandino in his book, *The Greatest Salesman in the World*. I read these books many times.

"The words of Thomas A. Edison especially helped me: 'Genius and success are one percent inspiration and ninety-nine percent perspiration.' Edison encouraged me to work hard."

Gil told me, "One of the first great speakers I ever heard in person was Dr. Wayne Dyer. I walked away from his program with a wonderfully simple yet powerful formula for achieving a goal. He taught us to ask ourselves four simple questions:

"'What is my goal?

"'What is stopping me from getting there?

"'What's the first step toward achieving my goal?

"'When am I going to take this first step?'

"These questions have been extremely instrumental in helping me analyze and achieve my goals. The voices of these great speakers, who I heard via an audio record, by reading books, and by attending their programs in person caused me to awaken and to take notice of all the road signs to the successful way of life."

Dianna Booher

One of the women speakers I admire most is Dianna Booher, M.A. Dianna is the author of twenty-five books on the subject of business communication. Her books cover the entire range of quality communication and improved productivity. Her material is so good that several of her titles have been selected by Book-of-the-Month/ Fortune Book Club and many others.

I like her practical, simple style that outlines effective ways to communicate with those at work and at home.

Dianna Booher
Top communication expert, author,
international speaker

The list of Dianna's clients read like the Who's Who of American Business. You may have seen her as she has been interviewed on over one thousand radio/TV talk shows.

Dianna told me that when she was a child, and then later as a young adult, she watched Art Linkletter interview the children on his television program segment, "Kids Say the Darndest Things." She said, "Art was never a taller man than when he sat down on the dais eye-to-eye with those kids. He picked their souls for profound truths."

Dianna loves Art's genuine warmth and sincerity, which she says came through to her even in his casual conversation. She sees Art Linkletter as the consummate communicator.

"Although at that time I didn't know what the skill involved, I realized he has the uncommon knack of entertaining all ages at once. In his unassuming, understated manner, with just the right pause, lifted eyebrow, puzzled look, follow-up probe or oral 'translation,' Art turns a child's answer into a profound truth for all the adults watching his show. Art Linkletter is the original, genuine Mr. Nice-Guy, on the platform," she explained.

We asked Dianna Booher, the magnificent communicator, to tell us her favorite quote. She said: "Whosoever shall seek to save his life shall lose it: and whosoever shall lose his life shall preserve it." —Jesus, recorded in Luke 17:33.

Dianna told me, "Dottie, if you take it seriously, speaking becomes a mission. Speakers who "lose" themselves communicating with an audience find themselves in others' lives quite often.

"Inspiring and inspired speakers discover they've changed others' lifestyles, their habits, their finances, and even their relationships with spouses and children. But most of all, great speakers find they have influenced their audience to fulfill their higher destinies."

Art Linkletter

Perhaps you have heard Art Linkletter on radio or seen him on television. He has been a TV and radio star for more than forty-five years.

Art Linkletter
World-famous and beloved radio/TV star,
author, speaker

He performed in two of the longest running shows in broadcast history: "House Party," daytime CBS-TV and radio, which won an Emmy Award for best daytime TV show and four Emmy nominations; "People are Funny" was featured on nighttime NBC-TV and radio for nineteen years. It was in the top ten rating list most of those years and won three Emmy nominations. Art also starred in numerous specials, two major motion pictures, and many TV dramas.

He has written twenty-three books, of which *Kids Say the Darndest Things* is my favorite. Art's newest bestseller is *Old Age Is not for Sissies*.

When you meet Art in person, the first impression you get is that here is an old and much loved friend. His manner of speech in person is just as you have seen and heard it on the media. He is a kind, witty man. Although Art is a busy, involved businessman with interests in oil, cattle, publishing, home building, land development, ranching, and manufacturing, and serves on half a dozen boards of directors, there is nothing about him that is not as down to earth as your next-door neighbor. He reminds me of the line from Rudyard Kipling's poem, "If." "If you can speak with princes or with paupers and treat those two imposters just the same... "

Art began interviewing children on his shows with his own son Jack when the boy was about four years old. When Jack grew up he had his own TV show called "On the Go," about unusual businesses. Jack brought his crew to my advertising office and interviewed me for his program.

Art Linkletter told me he has two favorite quotes which have meant much to him. The first is from famed UCLA basketball coach and wonderful speaker, John Wooden: "Things turn out best for the people who make the best of the way things turn out."

Art's second favorite quote is from Lowell Thomas, the great newscaster who encouraged Art to become a professional speaker when Art was about fifty-five years old. Lowell said: "You will find speaking easier the older you get. After seventy-five everything you say will remind you of something else!"

When I asked Art which great speaker first inspired him, he told me: "My first inspirational speaker, who

Marva Collins
Genius teacher/speaker, author *The Marva
Collins Way*

became one of my close friends, is Norman Vincent Peale. Twenty-five years ago, following the death of my daughter, he urged me to devote my talents to speaking in the field of drug abuse prevention. The wonderful stories in his books and speeches have been an inspiration to me to make my serious points through illustrative anecdotes.

"Dr. Peale reminded me that the Bible's greatest sermons were parables, generally about everyday people whose lives were changed by faith. In his mid '90s, he continues to inspire me with his warmth and understanding.

"I will never forget the tremendous moment when he was called upon to speak at an imposing formal funeral that was presided over by high-ranking priests and archbishops from the Catholic church. The strict liturgy and reading of Latin words was dramatically altered by the simple, plain, heart-spoken words of Dr. Peale, who brought the high-sounding ceremony down to earth with his warmth and humanity.

"I try to make everyone in my audience feel as if I am speaking with them. Not at, or to them, but with them, so that as I speak and can see them nod in agreement I know we are making contact on an intimate level. This of course is made possible by the microphone and loud speaker which enables today's speaker to modulate the voice tone from stentorian to a whisper. Fifty years of speaking to hundreds of millions of people on a microphone has given me the experience and knowledge to treat everyone as if each person were getting my total attention. It is why I never use notes or teleprompters, so as never to lose the eye contact so important to a speaker."

Art Linkletter is a great speaker in the full sense of Aristotle's description. Art told me, "Dottie, people are the same everywhere I speak. They mirror my friendly, accepting attitude."

Marva Collins

It was my delight to interview the great teacher, Marva Collins, for my *Sharing Ideas Newsmagazine*. We honored her as our "Consummate Speaker of the Year," with the help of Mr. Alan S. Walker of the Program Corporation of America Speakers Bureau.

Mr. Walker told us: "Marva Collins is a highly motivational speaker. She is one of the most inspiring, outspoken, and controversial figures in American education, one of the most brilliant teachers in American history. Many TV shows have featured her, including "Good Morning, America," the "Phil Donahue Show" and the "Hallmark Hall of Fame." Stories about her have been featured across the country and in *Time* and *Newsweek* magazines. Her personal example of courage and tenacity has opened new intellectual horizons for children everywhere."

After reading Marva's books, *The Marva Collins Way* and *Ordinary Children, Extraordinary Teachers*, I wanted to know more about this magnificent speaker, magical teacher, and most extraordinary woman. You may have seen the movie made about her life, The Marva Collins Story. She was portrayed by Cicely Tyson. Marva took her public schoolteacher's retirement money and built her own school in Chicago where she teaches children everyone else has given up on.

One of the many things that caught my interest about Marva Collins was that she quotes so many of my favorite friends of the mind. She begins each new class (pre-kindergarten on up) with this line from Ralph Waldo Emerson's, "Essay on Self-Reliance": "In every work of genius, we recognize our own rejected thoughts: they come back to us with a certain alienated majesty."

When I asked Marva why she begins classes for such young children with Emerson's "Self-Reliance" she told me, "You must believe in your own thoughts, because if you don't, somebody else will say what you were afraid to say. Nothing frustrates me more than people who say, 'You have to do it your way, don't you?'

"What they don't understand is, it is not doing it my way. Every expert blundered and made mistakes before they became an expert. You never get there if you depend on other people to do it for you."

Marva's school takes in children other schools reject, those labeled hopeless. Some have been told they are mentally retarded, have learning disabilities, or emotional problems. She loves them all, teaches them all, inspires them all. The waiting list for her inner-city Westside Preparatory School is over one thousand. Her students read books straight from college book lists, because she says that the old fashioned "See Spot Run" beginning reading books have nothing to catch the minds, intelligence, and hearts of children. I especially love her Creed, which all of her classes recite each morning:

The Marva Collins Creed

"I was born to win, if I do not spend too much time
trying to fail.

I can become a citizen of the world
if I do not spend too many energies attempting
to be local.

I will ignore the tags and names given me
by society, since only I know what I have
the ability to become.

I will continue to let others predict,
but only I can determine what I will, can, or cannot do."

Marva believes four-year-olds can learn to read and can understand Plato, Shakespeare, Goethe, and many more creative thinkers. She agrees with the great speaker/author Ralph Waldo Emerson. He said: "We carry the world in our head, the whole of astronomy and chemistry, suspended in a thought."

Marva told us: "Just look at the average four-year-old who watches a lot of TV. Television treats children like bright, reasoning people. Schools treat them like idiots. Just the opposite of what they can be. I find that fascinating. I just spoke to an audience of parents of a well-known company about raising brighter children. I told them about my three-year-old grandson. I had read a selection to him from Herman Melville's 'Moby Dick.' 'Everytime, in this slippery world, we all need something to hang on to.'

"When he got into a tenuous situation on the slide or the swing, I told him 'Sean, we're in a slippery world, we all need something to hang on to.'

"One day he was going down into my basement. There are no hand rails there. He looked at me and this three-year-old said, 'Grandma, you should put some banisters here! In this slippery world, we all need something to hang on to.'

"We feed our children on junk, trivia, and then say the children can't learn. It is too abstract for them. Anything abstract given long enough becomes concrete."

Marva was also inspired by another fascinating speaker, Ayn Rand, author of *Atlas Shrugged*. Marva told me: "We teach a lot of Ayn Rand's work, not just because she wrote it, but because I actually think that way. She talks about 'the creator doesn't live for anyone but themselves.' When I go to affairs and see everyone making business contacts, it is like a bunch of sycophants. It becomes rather nauseous after awhile, because everybody, I mean the 'second-hander' lives to be helped by the creator."

Marva Collins is a great, creative person who happens to speak well. Horace might have been speaking of her when he wrote in his Odes: "Instruction increases inborn worth, Right discipline strengthens the heart."

Jim Rohn
"America's Chairman of the Board," the
Emerson to business, author/writer,
powerful speaker

CHAPTER 8

Jim Rohn

Have you ever seen a miracle happen before your eyes? Many people are inspired to change their lives when they hear great speakers, but it usually doesn't show immediately on the outside. You only learn about it when you talk to them later in life after they have achieved great success.

When I first heard Jim Rohn speak, the audience was seated at tables of ten people. Next to me was a middle-aged woman who seemed agitated at the behavior of her rebellious teenage son. If you have teenagers in your life you will understand.

The boy was scrouched down so that his neck touched the back of the chair, his long legs were crossed at the ankle and stretched out so that no one could pass without stepping over him or tripping. His arms were folded across his chest, his chin down, and his lower lip stuck out belligerently.

His mother begged him to sit up, to pay attention. Evidently she had forced him to come. He was rude and withdrawn, determined to make the program as miserable for her (and everyone else) as he could.

Then Jim Rohn began to speak. Jim has a soft, humorous, pleasant but powerful style filled with stories. He tells tales of simple things like ants and how they never give up. He explained that you must act first. That God says, "If you don't move, I don't move."

When Jim said, "Everything we have and are, we attract by the person we become," the boy sat up a bit. Then a little more, until finally he was sitting erect. His mother and everyone else at the table held their breath.

The boy quickly asked his mother if she had a pen and paper in her purse! Then he began taking notes as fast as he could write and never stopped during the entire two hours. The magic moment of recognition had occurred. The boy caught the bright light of Jim's ideas, and realized they were true because he already knew them within his own heart and mind!

In beginning my little business on foot and building it step by step, I received criticism from many. I pulled my children in a wagon to the grocery store and hauled home crates to make my first desk and shelves. Neighbors and relatives said the old, usual things. "Who do you think you are?" "You can't do that, you have no college education!" "We won't let you in, you are only a woman." "My husband won't allow me to work." On and on, like a blaring radio, so loud it was hard to think.

What I heard Jim Rohn say that day I too recognized as my own inner truth: "If you sow, you can reap. You must sow first! Unless you change what you are, you will always have what you've got!"

What he said matched the tape in my head. Because Jim Rohn knew what I know, I could switch off the negative "ghetto-blaster" noise of the naysayers. It didn't matter what they said because they did not know who I was. They could only speak for themselves, not me.

Jim Rohn is a farm boy from Idaho who went to work at age twenty-five for a most unusual man named Earl Shoaff. Jim had attended a sales conference where Mr. Shoaff was the speaker. Jim reported that he was captivated by Earl Shoaff's ideas: "Keep a personal daily journal. Become a student of business skills. Study how to do well in the marketplace. Do better and better constantly. Be a pro in everything in life."

Jim gathered his courage after the program, walked up to Earl Shoaff, and introduced himself. Earl Shoaff recognized the inner light in Jim Rohn's eyes. He hired him and treated him like a son, spending hours teaching Jim his personal philosophy. Jim moved from salesperson to executive vice-president of the company.

Jim says, "Why did this great man appear at this point in my life? Why do good things happen when they do? For me, this is part of the mystery of life."

When Earl Shoaff died, Jim decided to pick up his mantle of author, speaker, teacher, and master inspirer. Today Jim Rohn's audio albums are recorded in seven languages. He is an internationally famous speaker, author of *The Five Major Pieces to the Life Puzzle, Success Strategies of Wealth & Happiness, The Seasons of Life,* and a four-video program, "How to Have Your Best Year Ever."

Here are comments on Jim Rohn's accomplishments by some of the great speakers in this book: Earl Nightingale, my dear friend, "Jim Rohn is the most compelling, inspirational, and results-oriented speaker of our time"; dynamic Tom Hopkins, "Jim Rohn is a modern-day Will Rogers"; brilliant Brian Tracy, "Jim Rohn is outstanding! He is among the most polished, professional speakers in America."

Jim wrote this in an introduction for one of my books: "All the successful movers and shakers with whom I have had contact are good readers. Their curiosity drives them. They simply have to know. They constantly seek new ways to become better. All leaders are readers. Today we also learn through the miracle of electronic publishing—through audio and video tapes. There are thousands of books and tapes on how to be a stronger, more decisive, effective leader and develop influence. Yet many do not use this wealth of knowledge. How do you explain that?

"Thousands of successful people have written and recorded their inspiring stories. Yet some people don't want to read or listen. They say, 'I struggle home, eat, watch a little TV, go to bed. I can't stay up half the night and *read.*' This is the sincere person who is behind on the bills. You can work hard and be sincere all of your life and still wind up broke, confused, and embarrassed.

"Devote just thirty minutes a day to learning. You want to really do well? Stretch your thirty minutes. All of us can afford to miss a few meals; none can afford to lose out on ideas, examples, and inspiration. Don't miss learning. Think of your reading time as 'tapping the treasure of ideas.' You are what you read."

Anthony Robbins

You may have read about Anthony Robbins as the seminar leader who taught his audience to literally walk on fire. His remarkable fire-walk program has been featured in the media of nineteen countries.

Anthony Robbins
Famed Fire Walk, international inspirational
speaker/author

Anthony Robbins had accomplished more by his early thirties than most people do in their entire lives. He is author of the book *Unlimited Power*, published in eleven languages with 750,000 copies sold. His newest book, *Awaken the Giant Within: How to Take Immediate Control of Your Mental, Emotional, Physical and Financial Destiny*, has taken off on the same tremendous success track. He has spoken to many big companies world wide and has filled stadiums with attendees for his seminars. He has been featured in *Life, Omni, Time, Newsweek,* and *SUCCESS* magazines, and top world newspapers. He founded nine companies and became a millionaire by the age of twenty-four.

The first impression I got of Anthony Robbins in person is that he is a very big man. A giant in spirit, personality, and his physical self. He has big hands and stands a powerful six feet, seven inches tall. He has his audience stand up, sit down, think, shout, move, as if he won't let them drift off away from the things he is teaching them. He insists they be alive and awake. Occasionally he hits his chest. Since he wears a hands-free radio mike, this produces a very loud bang(!) like an explosion. The first time he did this, I saw the whole audience jump!

In interviewing Anthony Robbins for my *Sharing Ideas Newsmagazine*, I asked, "Did you know that all the other speakers for the rest of the conference imitated you and hit their chests as they came up to the mike following your program? How did you begin that dramatic attention-getting action!"

Anthony told me, "Dottie, I hit the right-hand side of my chest. It communicates my number one method of what it takes to be an effective speaker. You have to have unbelievable passion about what you are communicating. I never sat down and thought, how can I do this? In my passion of performing I do things. When something works, I remember it.

"Once when I was making a point to an audience and was very intense about it, I smacked my chest and brought my other hand forward and up. I saw the whole audience just about jump out of their chairs!

"I continue to hit my chest as I speak because it makes me feel good. I do it for me more than the audience. I do it as an anchor that puts me in a powerful passionate state. The noise and movement express my intensity. Because the microphone is near my chest you can hear the explosive impact."

I asked Anthony if he rehearses his programs. "Dottie, I got several letters from an audience that said, 'You have a special gift—you delivered an inspired program. No one could have practiced that.' They are right. I don't practice my speeches.

"This is how I prepare. I go out with a very clear idea of what I want to do. I work hard, gathering as much information as possible. I create an outline in my mind. However, rarely does it end up exactly that way. I get up before the crowd and I absolutely trust in my Creator and my unconscious mind. I am totally and completely focused on delivering to my audience what they really need at that moment.

"That's why my speech changes sometimes. I am out there on stage looking at how people respond. I watch my audience very closely. I have so much passion that it just flows. Unlimited examples of stories flow through me at any moment."

This most unusual young man told me his favorite quote is by Orison Swett Marden, the first publisher of *SUCCESS* magazine: "Deep within us dwell slumbering powers: Powers that would astonish us, that we never dreamed of possessing. Forces that could revolutionize our life, turn it around and put it into action."

When I asked Anthony which speaker inspired him, he told me, "Jim Rohn, my first personal development teacher, who always taught me that if you have enough reasons, you can do anything."

Anthony was inspired when he read Napoleon Hill's book, *Think and Grow Rich*. He is an avid reader. He told me, "If you want to increase the quality of your life, add to your 'profound knowledge information.' You will find in a book virtually any answer you ever wanted, or knowledge of any question for which you seek. Books are the greatest treasure that we have."

Anthony Robbins attended the same high school in Glendora, California, where our children graduated. When he was seventeen, Anthony was invited to attend a seminar presented by Jim Rohn. He spent his entire week's pay on the ticket. Anthony told me, "I was blown away. Jim Rohn talked about all the books I had read. I got so excited! I wanted to make a difference in the world.

"From that night on I began to set goals. I used the Rohn technique to write a plan. Then I went back to the Jim Rohn seminar and convinced him I could do a job for him selling tickets to his seminars. I slept in my Volkswagen and convinced the bank to lend me twelve hundred dollars to live on, more than the car was worth. I got extremely inspired and began to do well. I was the youngest guy who sold tickets for Jim Rohn's seminars. That is how my speaking began. I became their top salesman in a month.

"Then I grew." (Surely an understatement of greatest magnitude!) Anthony Robbins told me he plans to become President of the United States. Keep your eye on this big young man with the gigantic dreams.

Naomi Rhode

One of the great women speakers I admire is Naomi Rhode, 1994 president of the National Speakers Association. She and her brilliant husband, Jim, began their speaking careers with a focus on the world of dentistry. They have also developed a gorgeous color catalog of products for dentists which began in a fascinating way.

Jim Rhode told me, "We were convinced that dental offices needed uplifting, positive reinforcement for patients and staff. The dentists complained that they could not find posters which accomplished this need. We brought together the best posters we could buy and presented them in a new way, as a continuity subscription program, our "Poster Club." The dentists receive eighteen new posters, designed especially for them, four times a year. A bit like Book-of-the-Month Club.

Naomi Rhode
President, National Speakers Association,
internationally famous author/speaker

Many speakers develop products. The Rhodes have created ten audiocassette albums and two books. However, their dental catalog produces well over twenty million dollars in sales annually. Their newest project is to develop and produce twelve major catalogs per year, for veterinarians, physicians, eye care professionals, etc. An amazing story.

Naomi is a role model because she not only is a great speaker, she is a great woman in every sense of the word. She and her husband have created a most unique and successful business, and they have a beautiful family of children and grandchildren. The Rhodes speak together ninety percent of the time.

Naomi says, "My husband and I feel we are at our best when we are speaking together. We combine the power of left and right brain hemisphere themes of our lives. Jim's entrepreneurial business expertise and my concern and love for sharing of excellence, communication/ interpersonal relationship skills, and inspiration lead to our synergy on the platform.

"A strong part of our story has been the inclusion of our children in our seminars for at least thirteen of our eighteen years of speaking. During the summers we give child and teenage seminars to the children of our participants. Our children are now grown, married, and each one uses their speaking skills in a specific way."

Naomi and Jim remind me of one of my favorite quotes by Booker T. Washington, the great educator: "The world cares very little about what a man or woman knows: It is what the man or woman is able to do that counts. Excellence is to do a common thing in an uncommon way."

Naomi Rhode was inspired by her father, Virgil Asbury Reed, an ordained Methodist minister who later in life became a professional Boy Scout executive, speaking for that wonderful organization.

Naomi says, "His storytelling ability was flawless. To watch him speak and change an audience to action via an elevated life perspective was amazing for me as a young woman. I had no idea that I would ever become a professional speaker myself. It was not only a genetic gift that was passed on, but an environmental aura of the

Jack Canfield
Top U.S. self-esteem expert, author,
international speaker

power of persuasive speech and the magic of words which has been a guiding light for me in my professional career.

"Though he died when I was only thirteen years old, I am privileged to have many of his speech notes, his books, and the ongoing testimonies of people who still come to me with stories of the changes he engendered by his platform presence. My favorite quote is from my father: 'They say what they say, let them say.'"

"My favorite story is one he told about Lan Yeppe. Give everything you are paid for, and just a little extra. This is the motto of our company."

Jack Canfield

When Jack Canfield attended one of my seminars here at our ranch in Glendora, California, he was fascinated with the big, old-fashioned, oak and tile soda fountain in my personal office. He loved the story of how it came to be here and wrote to me afterwards, "I wish we were next-door neighbors, Dottie. I would come over to your house and sit on one of those soda fountain stools every day for fifteen or twenty minutes and we could talk about the world of professional speaking."

I was honored when Jack made our soda fountain famous. He told about it in one of his great audio albums for the Nightingale-Conant Company. Jack is president and chairman of the board of the Foundation for Self-Esteem and a director of the Optimum Performance Training Institute.

Jack was appointed by the California State Legislature to the historic California Task Force to Promote Self-Esteem, Personal & Social Responsibility. He has conducted intensive personal and professional development seminars for over six hundred thousand people worldwide. Not only has he spoken for corporations, schools, colleges, and all kinds of governmental agencies, he has been seen by millions more on national TV shows such as "The Today Show," "BBC," and "NBC Nightly News." Jack is a member of the editorial boards of three professional journals and several newsletters. He has authored many books and audiocassettes, too numerous to list here. His most recent video production was created by Chesney Productions in Irvine, California. Jack's forty-five-minute presentation on, "A Blueprint for a Winning Life" was included in the program "Seven Magnificent Motivational Speakers," which you may have seen, as it is marketed nationally via cable television.

The thing that impresses me most about Jack is his humble, loving attitude. He seems to me to be the personification of his own favorite quote by Leo Buscaglia: "Love is life. And if you miss love, you miss life."

The speaker who most inspired Jack Canfield to become a speaker himself is the Reverend Jesse Jackson. Jack tells this story in his programs: "I was a high school teacher in an inner city school in Chicago. A fellow teacher invited me to his church on Sunday. Having grown up a Presbyterian, I had never heard the impassioned preaching of a Baptist preacher. I was mesmerized by the passion, emotion, and deep commitment to love, justice, and harmony—all the values I espoused.

"The Reverend Jackson's oratorical skills moved me deeply, as they did everyone else in the congregation. I remember thinking, I want to touch people deeply and move them in the same way. In those days Jesse would always end his sermon by having the audience repeat: 'I am somebody! I may be black, but I am somebody. I may be poor, but I am somebody. I may be uneducated, but I am somebody.'"

Jack sums up his work in this way: "It is probably no accident that the focus of my work has been self-esteem and empowerment. I have dedicated my life to having everybody I teach, touch, or reach through my books and tapes leave with the feeling that they too are somebody. That they can make their deepest, most heart-felt dreams come true, if they only make the effort.

"I realize that the source of all love starts with self-love and self-acceptance. I believe peace between people and peace among nations starts with peace within one's self."

Recently Jack Canfield and dynamic speaker Mark Victor Hansen wrote a most marvelous and unusual book, *Chicken Soup for the Soul: 101 Stories to Awaken the Heart and Rekindle the Spirit* (Health Communications, Inc.) which was an immediate bestseller. I was delighted to be one of the 101 people whose stories were included.

Jack Canfield reminds me of one of my favorite quotes by my friend of the mind who I met at the little library in the chicken ranching rural town of Baldwin Park, California,—Albert Einstein: "Try not to become a person of success, but rather, try to become a person of value."

Mark Victor Hansen

I knew Mark Victor Hansen a long time before I had the privilege of hearing him speak. He is an energetic, charismatic young man who speaks with the eloquence of William Jennings Bryan. The National Speakers Association had appointed Nido Qubein to chair their convention in San Diego. However, Nido's first baby decided to arrive that very weekend. So Mark Victor Hansen was called in to replace him on very short notice.

Hearing Mark that day made a difference in my life. We all have ebbs and flows. My creativity was at low ebb that day and I was feeling a bit blue. But as Mark spoke, holding the audience in absolute thrall, I suddenly had a vision of creating a new audio album to help all of the beginning speakers who ask me for advice.

I decided to call it, "How to Enter the world of Paid Speaking." I had not considered such a project until that moment. That audio album has become quite famous and has been featured many times in *SUCCESS* magazine.

Some of the things Mark said which influenced me that day were: "Be on-purpose to do something significant and world-serving. It puts all the forces of the universe at your service. Assuming your goal or objective is big enough, the God factor comes to serve us. We think right, act right, and commence doing the right things for the right reasons... and we get all the right results, right here, right now."

Mark's story was featured recently in *SUCCESS* magazine. When he began his business he had money for a tiny office, but none for an apartment. So he slept on the floor by his desk. He never gave up.

Mark Victor Hansen
Mr. Energy! author, international
inspirational speaker

Mark Victor Hansen speaks to thousands of people in the corporate world and national trade and professional associations, plus educational and philanthropic institutions around the world. His best-selling book, *Future Diary*, features goal-setting techniques. He has been featured on many national and international television interviews and has recorded a number of excellent audiocassette albums.

Recently while the famous Australian speaker/singer/composer Michele Blood visited America, she heard Mark Victor Hansen speak. I asked her what she thought of his presentation. Michele told me, "Dottie, Mark has a natural spiritual quality and energy. He lives in joy and shares it completely. No one failed to listen to him for one single second."

One of my favorite Mark Victor Hansen stories is about how he met actor Paul Hogan (Crocodile Dundee) while Mark was flying to Australia for a series of speaking engagements.

Mark says, "What a promoter! Hogan did all those 'Wonder-Down-Under' TV commercials free. First for his country and second because he knew he had to become famous in the U.S. before he could be big-time all over the world. After the commercials had the people in America wanting more, he came out with his movie *Crocodile Dundee*. While some people say, 'I won't do anything unless I am paid for it,' Paul Hogan had a very different idea. He is a self-actualizer. The great ones understand about planting seeds. Paul began as a bridge painter. His friends insisted he try out his comedy on a new TV amateur hour show called 'New Faces.' He was not paid a fee. That show opened up his TV career."

When I asked Mark who had first inspired him, he told me, "Dottie, Dr. R. Buckminster Fuller was my great and inspiring teacher who thought, taught, and lived on a grand scale.

"'Bucky,' as he was affectionately called, was a self-made Renaissance man, the Leonardo da Vinci of our time. He chose to be a human guinea pig and discover what one man could do in one human lifetime. Fuller's quest was to: 'Make the world work for one hundred percent of humanity.'

"As a result, when he spoke, Fuller was deeply interesting, street-smart, enchantingly comprehensive, and wise beyond the mere words he used. His language was what was called "Fulleresque" because he had mastered eight diverse disciplines and interfaced them in a comprehensive framework, so everyone understood a newer, bigger picture.

"Fuller inspired listeners like myself to think from a comprehensive, anticipatory design-science viewpoint. He made true believers out of his listeners and taught us to awaken to the fact that individually we could make a difference. We could make the world work, physically and economically, for everyone."

Mark says, "My favorite quote by Dr. Fuller, who wrote *I Seem to Be a Verb,* is 'I'm dedicated to humanity's comprehensive welfare on Spaceship Earth.'"

Mark explains, "Fuller, in my imagination, is the ideal speaker because he was an insider on the universe. The titles that he carried in his lifetime include: architect, artist, author, poet, scientist, philosopher, speaker, educator, inventor, entrepreneur, businessman, philanthropist, and human treasure. He was the ideal all high-minded speakers aspire to.

"Fuller said: 'Those who came and learned, leave to do great things. Those who don't are called disciples.'"

In our next chapter we will talk about another famous Californian, our former governor who became President of the United States, Ronald Reagan, the "great communicator."

Rev. Robert Schuller
Builder of Crystal Cathedral, "Hour of Power"
TV program, world-famous inspirational
speaker, author

Chapter 9

Dr. Robert Schuller

People in my audiences all over the world ask me about the Crystal Cathedral in Garden Grove, California. I have spoken at seminars there and have attended many times, especially to hear Dr. Norman Vincent Peale when he spoke. I have always felt a close bond with the Schuller family and love to hear Dr. Robert Schuller tell his audiences about their beginnings. Robert and Arvella and their two small children drove to southern California hoping to start a new church at about the same time I pushed my two babies in that dilapidated baby stroller, searching for the *Baldwin Park Bulletin* office.

The Schullers, like me, were very low on money. But they are the kind of people who do not look at difficulties, they look for opportunities. When they reached southern California, Dr. Schuller made a list of all the buildings they might rent. School buildings, mortuary chapels, community buildings, and synagogues. They even thought of one of the popular new drive-in movie theaters springing up in the southland.

The young couple were turned down everywhere. The Orange Drive-In Theater was the last possibility on their list. Each car had it's own radio system, which stood on a stand in the huge parking space.

I well remember that theater. I passed it often as I sold advertising and built my business in that same area. Robert and Arvella first considered using the snack bar area for services, but there were no chairs. Then Robert Schuller got an idea. He asked the theater owner if he could stand on the roof of the snack bar where he could be seen throughout the huge parking lot and speak over the sound system piped in to the cars. The owner of the drive-in theater agreed. The rent for Sunday morning for the church service was ten dollars.

The Schullers built a wooden cross and set it up on the roof of the snack bar with a lectern in front of it for

Dr. Schuller and made a place for Arvella to play her small organ, which they carried home after each service.

Would people want to sit in their cars to go to church? It had never been done before. The Schullers wrote wonderful advertising copy for flyers, inviting worshipers to come and meet together surrounded by orange groves where they could see the beautiful snow-capped California mountains in the distance. Their slogan was: "Worship as you are, in the family car." Then the couple went door to door in the surrounding areas inviting people to come.

Dr. Schuller began his first service with the words, "If you have faith as a grain of mustard seed... " Forty-six cars filled with people attended. Many with little children, some with elderly or incapacitated people who could not go to church. The new church at the Orange Drive-In Theater certainly had room to expand. There was space for seventeen hundred cars.

What a contrast with their Crystal Cathedral church of today, located right across the freeway from the old Orange Drive-In Theater. It is constructed in the shape of a four-point star. It is 207 feet at its widest point and is 415 feet long. It is built of steel set with 10,600 glass windows. Those inside can look up and out at the beautiful California mountains and at night can see the stars above them in the firmament. The feature of a drive-in for cars is retained and is still very popular. Two ninety-foot high doors open so that those sitting outside in their cars can attend and hear Dr. Schuller speak. The Crystal Cathedral is unique, unusual, and breathtakingly beautiful.

At this lovely location are held gigantic Christmas and Easter pageants and many educational and seminar programs. A separate building houses a very large bookstore. Dr. Schuller's wonderful "Hour of Power" television programs are broadcast literally all over the world.

The Crystal Cathedral reminds me of one of my favorite Schuller quotes, which certainly describes this remarkable family: "Excellence is the motto of great people."

I bought one of Dr. Schuller's posters at that early time when I was struggling so hard to get my business going. I hung it up in my tiny home office. These words gave me great courage:

The Possibility Thinker's Creed

"When I am faced with a mountain
I will not quit.
I will keep on trying until I climb over,
Find a path through, tunnel underneath,
Or simply stay and turn the mountain into a gold mine,
with God's help."

The "Possibility Thinker's Creed" is part of Dr. Schuller's famous book, *Move Ahead with Possibility Thinking*. The poster of the creed has inspired people world wide.

Our great friend, author/speaker Rev. Roger Hoath of England asked Dr. Schuller about his most meaningful, most beloved quote. Dr. Schuller said he saw it hanging on the wall in Dr. Norman Vincent Peale's office: "It is better to attempt something great and fail, than to attempt nothing and succeed."

Dr. Schuller reported that the three speakers who influenced him most were: Billy Graham, who inspired him to bring his "Hour of Power" program to television in 1969 during Graham's Anaheim crusade; Dr. Norman Vincent Peale; and Bishop Fulton Sheen.

Dr. Schuller has written over thirty books. Four of these are *New York Times* best-sellers. They have been translated into twenty-two foreign languages.

Billy Graham, Dr. Peale, and many, many other famous speakers and celebrities have spoken and/or sung at the Crystal Cathedral. He is a giant, who arrived to tell us all the ideas we needed so much, "Tough times never last, tough people do."

I am proud to be among the millions who have taken courage from Robert and Arvella Schuller.

President Ronald Reagan

We Californians know Ronald Reagan as an old friend. He has served as president of the Screen Actors Guild in

President Ronald Reagan

President of the United States, Governor of State
of California, the "Great Communicator"

Hollywood and has made many pictures here, from that early one about "The Gipper," to the TV western series he hosted for "20 Mule Team Borax." We began to think of him as a great speaker about the time he ran for governor of our state.

I met him in Sacramento in his governor's office, when I attended a session with a delegation from our city of Glendora. I remember thinking how unassuming, humorous, and kind he was as we all clamored to have our pictures taken with him. There was nothing of arrogance or pompousness about Ronald Reagan. We felt we were in the presence of an old and trusted friend.

It was when he ran for President that we began to call him "the great communicator." One of the lines that I cherish from his many speeches is, "Each and every day is an opportunity to enrich our lives immeasurably by enlisting in the service of some good that is larger than our individual selves. If enough of us seized that opportunity on any one day... and never let it go, our lives, our nation, our world, would be forever changed."

President Reagan always remembered everyone he worked with and answered every letter. An example of his abundant caring and appreciation for those around him is this letter, which he wrote to his chief speech writer, Aram Bakshian, Jr. We published the story in *Sharing Ideas Newsmagazine*. "Your exceptional talents—creativity, eloquence, and wit—have been invaluable to me in communicating our message at home and abroad. You understand better than anyone else that leadership is not just making decisions, but explaining them clearly and persuasively."

After President Reagan left office I fully realized how much he is loved all over the world. My husband Bob and I were meeting friends for dinner at a San Diego hotel which overlooks the beautiful bay. We headed for the elevator to take us to the restaurant at the top of the building. However, we could scarcely get across the lobby. It was shoulder-to-shoulder full of people laden with suitcases, talking in many foreign languages.

Dorothea Johnson
CEO, Protocol School, Washington, D. C.,
international speaker, world expert
on international manners

As we stood and waited for the overburdened elevator, I heard two men behind me speaking with a Scot's burr. I turned and smiled at them and said, "Welcome to America! Why are all of you people here?"

They explained that the international builders' convention they were attending had taken every room in every hotel in downtown San Diego. Shuttles came to the front of the hotel every fifteen minutes to take them to the convention center.

"You must have a great keynote speaker for your convention!" I commented.

"Aye, yes, we have come to hear him. 'Tis President Ronald Reagan. He has promised to give us photographic opportunities after his talk. We have all brought cameras."

Dorothea Johnson

Dorothea is a very unusual woman. She is beautiful, charming, and offers the most unusual service. She is director of the Protocol School of Washington, D.C., where she provides protocol/etiquette services and cross cultural training to businesses, governments, and individuals from around the world. But above all, she teaches and personifies graciousness.

She is protocol consultant to the World Trade Center, Washington D.C., and protocol consultant and liaison to the Washington Diplomatic Community for the School of Attaché Training, Defense Intelligence College in Washington. Dorothea is the author of the column "International Protocol" featured in the *Washington Trade Report*. You may have read about her in *Newsweek* and many other publications.

The greats of all nations come to learn from this charming lady. She reminds me of what my grandmother said: "Politeness is to do and say the kindest thing, in the kindest way."

Dorothea's favorite quotation is from interior designer George Whitehurst, as he spoke about designers and talent. "There are those who share their talents and make money, and those who are incredibly talented but take

Dave Carey
U.S. pilot held prisoner five years in Vietnam.
Inspirational/humorist business speaker

those talents to their grave—poor. I want to know what are you going to do with what you know?"

Dorothea told me the speaker who most inspired her is Dr. Hester Beall Provensen, J.D., M.A., the honorary member and consultant of the Capital Speakers Club started in 1945 at the White House while Mrs. Harry S. Truman was First Lady. Dr. Provensen schedules two classes a year. Graduates are invited to join the Capital Speakers Club.

Dorothea reported that Dr. Beall Provensen possessed the platform and never lost a beat as she talked about public speaking as "an art which has to be studied." She remarked about the importance of posture. "Never lean on anything. If you do, you lose ninety-nine percent of your power."

To a member whose drooping shoulders were not to her liking, Dr. Provensen said, "Now see here, honey, I want you to carry yourself like you are paid a million bucks to speak, and they got a bargain."

Dave Carey

If any one of us had faced an experience as a POW of the Vietnamese—starved, beaten, tortured—and with no way of knowing how long we would be locked up, how many of us would emerge positive, full of humor, and a dynamic powerful speaker?

As his mind teetered on the edge of insanity because of repeated beatings and torture, Captain Carey was unable to move. The pain was excruciating. However, Dave says the agony of his mind was worst of all.

Then suddenly, he remembered a quotation from Sunday school. A line from the Twenty-third Psalm came into his head: "The Lord is my shepherd, I shall not want." If I can just remember all of the lines, I will regain my sanity, he thought.

It took Dave two days to recall all the words from his childhood, but he did accomplish this task, and in doing so brought his mind back to an even keel. Which proves that every good thought we have ever heard is still in our subconscious.

It was five long years of uncertainty and pain in prison before he was released and able to come home to his sweetheart and his family. Dave has many favorite quotes. One of them is also one of mine. Winston Churchill said to the world via radio when England was being smashed by Nazi bombs, "Never give up. Never Give up. Never give up!"

Churchill later remarked about those words: "I was not the lion. But it fell to me to give the lion's roar. The price of greatness is responsibility."

Listen to what Dave Carey says in his speeches about surviving his experience: "We did what we had to do. We did our best. We kept our sense of humor. We chose to grow. We kept the faith in ourselves, our faith in each other, our faith in our country, and our faith in God."

I am especially inspired by Dave's message that faith is crucial to our survival. He says: "Commitment, faith, friendship, and mutual support are the keystones to a meaningful life. Success comes not so much as a result of overcoming adversity, but as a result of using it creatively." He speaks about searching for and finding humor in emotional chaos and using it to effect positive changes in our lives. When the Vietnamese captors asked Dave for details of his missions he says, "I made up targets, bombing times, and tactics. When they asked me for the names in my squadron, I gave them the lineup of the Pittsburgh Pirates."

Dave Carey has had a distinguished career as a naval officer with extensive command experience. He is the recipient of the Legion of Merit, Bronze Star, Meritorious Service, Purple Heart, Navy Commendation, and many other awards and honors. He served as site director of the U.S.N. Leadership and Management Education/Training program.

The speaker who inspired Dave Carey is one of the great speakers in this book, Jim Rohn. Dave says, "Jim's style is very down to earth. He knows what he is talking about and he's not flamboyant. His advice is not in the get-rich-quick category, but rather that you have to pay your dues. You have to work and be patient. There is no easy way. On top of all that, Jim's advice works!"

And so does the advice of the humorous, inspirational, practical, great speaker Dave Carey.

Steve Ritchie

Another great American patriot who is a great speaker is Brigadier General. Steve Ritchie, U.S.A.F.R. Steve made aviation history when he downed five MiG-21s on his second tour of duty in Southeast Asia. He thereby became the only American pilot ever to shoot down five Soviet MiG-21s.

Steve is a veteran of 339 combat missions. His decorations include the Air Force Cross, four Silver Stars, ten Distinguished Flying Crosses, and twenty-five Air Medals. He is a command pilot with more than three thousand flying hours and eight hundred combat hours.

When I listen to him speak I am so proud to be an American. One of his stories is about one pilot who was downed in Vietnam and how all of the planes in all of the services combined to search for that one man.

I agree with C. Mickey Skinner, president of the Hershey Pasta Group, who wrote about Colonel Ritchie's speech: "I consider myself to be a pretty tough old bird, but you brought tears to my eyes on more than one occasion during your presentation."

Who inspires Steve Ritchie? Steve told me, "Dottie, I've been a fan and student of Paul Harvey since grade school. I managed to stay at home after lunch during fifth period study hall in my senior year in high school to listen to Paul Harvey's daily radio show.

"I wrote to him in February 1968 and asked if he'd be interested in hearing from a fighter pilot in Vietnam on a regular basis. He called me. I flew to Chicago. We've been friends ever since. He has had more influence on my philosophy and thinking than any single person in my life."

Paul Harvey is a famous speaker. Perhaps you have had the privilege of being in his audience in person. Here is one of Paul Harvey's ideas which especially inspires Steve Ritchie: "Throughout history, when people have been free, they became prosperous. After a period of prosperity they become lazy. They then ask the

Brigadier General Steve Ritchie, U.S.A.F., Retired
Top Gun Pilot Award, Vietnam.
Expert inspirational, patriotic speaker/author

government to do for them what they used to do and should do for themselves."

Gene Harrison

Col. Gene Harrison, Retired, commanded over four thousand troops in Vietnam. He was often sent out to bring up the morale of units who had heavy losses. I am so moved when I hear him talk about how he always goes out and talks to the men as they work: gets under the truck with them, has coffee with them, gets to know them, and then identifies the real problem so that it can be solved. No wonder his subject today is team building and development of individual leadership skills to enhance team effectiveness.

I never tire of hearing him do his hilarious routine about hunting dogs in the bayous of Florida and Mississippi. He barks like the dogs, plays all the parts of the hunters, and is so funny he has the audience wiping their eyes while they roar with laughter.

He headed the personnel policy section for the 185,000-person Marine Corps in Washington, D.C. While on this duty, one of his assistants was Oliver North, who is also a speaker. Today Gene is a famous speaker and consultant to a wide range of clients.

Gene Harrison reports that his favorite quote that inspired him as he began his speaking career is similar to one's first love: it will always be memorable and has an impact on what follows. "I heard Joel Weldon present his 'Elephants Don't Bite' program at the National Speakers Association. Here is the line which meant so much to me: 'What you value is what you think about. What you think about is what you become.'"

Gene wrote to us, "As to the speaker who grabbed my heart and never let go, the one who inspired me? Dottie, that speaker was you!

"I met you at a speaker's meeting and attended one of your training sessions on how to get started in the speaking profession. I had experience to share but did not know how to polish the presentations, choose my market, or develop materials. You spoke from the heart,

Colonel Gene Harrison, U.S. Marine Corps, Retired

Rose from private to head of Personnel Policy Section for 185,000-person Marine Corps in Washington, D.C.

demonstrated how to draw word pictures, and exemplified the mastery of the use of quotes and storytelling par excellence.

"From that point on, you became my source of knowledge about the speaking business, my inspiration and mentor."

Dana LaMon

I must add another hero to this chapter, Dana LaMon. Dana is an African American who lost his sight as a very young boy. He never let his blindness stop him for a moment. He worked hard and earned his law degree. He speaks, as Paul says in the New Testament, "with the voice of men and of angels" and with love. So much so, that Toastmasters International named him their "World Champion of Public Speaking." Dana LaMon reminds me of one of my favorite quotes: "Make no little plans, they have no power to stir men's blood. Make big plans: aim high in hope and work." —Daniel H. Burham.

Dana told me his favorite quotation, the one that has inspired him most of all, by Robert F. Kennedy: "Some men see things that are, and ask why? I see things that are not yet, and ask why not?"

Although he never sat in an audience to hear him speak in person, Dana is most moved by the speeches of Dr. Martin Luther King, Jr.

"My spine tingles as I listen to recordings of his work. He demonstrates a keen sense of human nature and what moves an individual. He has a powerful command of the English language, being able to communicate with the uneducated as well as the educated. His genuineness and sincerity are evident in all that he says. When I need inspiration, I pop an audio cassette of Dr. King's speeches into the player."

To close this chapter I add one of own favorite Dr. King quotes that has special meaning to me as a businesswoman who struggled hard to get started at a time women faced discrimination.

"When we let freedom ring... when we let it ring from every village and every hamlet, from every state and every

Dana La Mon
Blind attorney, inspirational speaker, recipient
Toastmasters' "World Champion
Public Speaking" Award

city, we will be able to speed up that day when all of God's children, black and white, Jews and Gentiles, Protestants and Catholics, will be able to join hands and sing in the words of that old Negro spiritual: Free at last! Free at last! Thank God Almighty, we are free at last!"
—Dr. Martin Luther King, Jr.

Steve Allen
Multi-talented comedian, musician,
author, actor, speaker

Chapter 10

Steve Allen

Andy Williams says, "If all of Steve Allen's talents were listed separately, they would take up the entire yellow pages of the Hollywood telephone directory!" Steve is the author of forty-two books including *How to Make a Speech* (McGraw-Hill). He stars in musical productions such as "Cinderella"; has made many movies like the "Benny Goodman Story"; composed over four thousand songs; composed scores for Broadway and television musical productions; is the original host of the "Tonight Show"; created, wrote, and hosted the "Meeting of the Minds" Emmy award-winning PBS-TV television series which received the Mort Adler Encyclopedia Britannica Award; and has received so many other honors and awards that this book could not encompass them all. Steve Allen is today's Renaissance man. I was honored to interview him for my magazine, *Sharing Ideas*.

In the 1920s, '30s, and '40s, the single most talented individual in the entertainment world was Noel Coward, the actor, vocalist, pianist, author, composer, lyricist, and director. Noel Coward described Steve Allen as "the most talented man in America."

In his wonderful book, *How to Make a Speech,* Steve Allen says, "The brain starts working the moment you are born, and never stops until you stand up to speak in public!"

Steve Allen sparkles. He answers questions from the audience, which bring howls of laughter. Examples:

Q. "How do you do all those wonderful things?"

A. "I like to use Noel Coward's answer to that same question: 'Brilliantly!'"

Q. "How do you keep looking so young?"

A. "I make it a point to hang around with old people!"

He often closes his program by bringing tears to the eyes of the audience with thrilling, virtuoso piano renditions of his most popular songs: "This Could Be the Start of Something Big," "Picnic," "Impossible," and the

Hermine Hilton
Author, *The Executive Memory Guide,*
exciting international
memory expert

"South Rampart Street Parade." He received long and heartfelt standing ovations.

I treasure Steve Allen's outlook on creativity. Steve believes that the mind does not get "tired." It just grows stale on one thing. He uses audio cassette recorders to dictate his plays, manuscripts, projects, letters, books, and music.

When one project lags, Steve lays down that cassette recording device, picks up another, and proceeds. No problem. He explains to his audiences, "The ability to write music on a score has nothing at all to do with musical creativity, any more than being able to type means an author has talent."

Steve Allen does not write his music. He composes on the piano and records his work.

One of Steve's favorite speakers is the late editor and author, Norman Cousins. Steve says there was nothing of a formal debater about Cousins. His voice was not deep and resonant. He even had a faint suggestion of a lisp. But Norman Cousins came over to his audience as the possessor of remarkable sincerity, conviction, and—at moments—a passionate intensity.

I have just received a letter from Steve Allen's office which contains more good news. He has just become abbot of the world-famed Friars Club, succeeding Milton Berle, and has been inducted into the TV Academy's Hall of Fame. Aristotle described Steve perfectly in his definition: "A great speaker is a great person who happens to speak well."

Hermine Hilton

Known as "America's Memory Motivator," Hermine is a funny, witty, and exciting performer who teaches her audiences a much-needed skill: How to remember. She is also a famous lyricist, dancer, and international speaker, perhaps best known as the author of *The Executive Memory Guide*, several excellent audio programs, and a new program "Namemoniks."

Hermine has her audience enthusiastically laughing and participating while she teaches them how to count in Japanese, or remember a long series of numbers. Then she delivers this blockbuster line, "Don't try to memorize. We must get the intelligence involved!"

What a profound statement. Anyone can memorize. Learning how to remember, to think, and then how to use what you remember—that is a real skill.

Hermine was a young ballet student of the great Russian choreographer, Bronislava Nijinska (sister of the famed dancer Nijinsky). Hermine tells her audiences that Madame Nijinska spoke in Russian, which was translated by her husband as she directed the brilliant dancers of the Ballet Russe and New York City Ballet. One day Madame Nijinska directed the other dancers to observe Hermine. She said, "You watch Hermine. It is not enough to know the steps; you must show the audience that the heart is dancing them."

This is equally true about speakers. It is not enough to know the words; the heart must believe them.

Hermine tells a story about the legendary entertainer Sammy Davis, Jr. "Sammy spoke before the Composers and Lyricists Guild, using excerpts from his powerful book, *Yes I Can*. He spoke directly from the heart. I went out and bought his book and devoured it, telling myself I can, too! Years later he recorded the TV theme from 'Hawaii Five-O' ('You Can Count On Me'), for which I wrote the lyrics."

The quotation which most moved Hermine comes from her own mother, Augusta. "She had a most lovely command of English and a voracious appetite for the printed word." Hermine explains, "She loved to remind me she'd once worked for Anita Luce, author of *Gentlemen Prefer Blondes*. My mother's speaking talent appeared late in life when she began giving book reviews for senior citizens. I called her the 'Grandma Moses' of the literary set. She sprinkled her speech with energy and motivation, prompting me to be always alert to possibilities. She encouraged me to enter a 'Quiz Kids' essay contest (and win) when I was nine.

"It was her reading about mnemonics, the study of memory, which interested me in becoming a speaker on this subject. Her most important message, which my mother used in her programs, has become a third-generation quote. When our daughter Espree graduated from middle school as valedictorian, she quoted my mother, her grandmother. 'Seize the opportunity of a life time during the lifetime of the opportunity.'"

Jack Anderson

Jack Anderson is America's foremost investigative reporter, speaker, and leader of the International Platform Association, founded before the Civil War by Daniel Webster. For forty-six years Jack has exposed government waste, deceit, and corruption. Millions of readers rely on his "Washington Merry-Go-Round" column distributed to more than six hundred major newspapers. Not only is Jack a world renowned speaker, he is bureau chief of *Parade Magazine,* host of "Jack Anderson's Watch on Washington," host of his own syndicated radio show, and publisher of the bimonthly business and financial newsletter, *Jack Anderson Confidential.*

The International Platform Association honored Jack with their Abraham Lincoln Award. Their first programs featured Andrew Jackson and Ralph Waldo Emerson at Milbury, Massachusetts. The famous Lincoln/Douglas debates were part of their Chautauqua section.

Jack Anderson began writing at age twelve as a Boy Scout reporter for the Scout page of the *Deseret News,* the number two daily newspaper in Utah. He learned how to write newscopy from real working reporters. Jack says it was good journalism. "I had to take the issues that affected our state and reduce them down to the level of a twelve-year-old."

Jack got his first big break when he was hired as a reporter for Drew Pearson, the famous columnist. Jack was chosen from one hundred applicants because he was the only one who had been a war correspondent. Drew Pearson's father, Paul Pearson, and Drew's grandfather, ran the "Swathmore Chautauqua Circuit" sending speakers all over the country via the railroads.

Jack Anderson explains his moniker "muckraker" as one which has always been given to investigative reporters. It was first used by Teddy Roosevelt in regard

Jack Anderson
Famous investigative reporter, speaker, author,
national newspaper column, "Washington
Merry-Go-Round," and many books

to Sinclair Lewis, who exposed scandals. That upset Teddy Roosevelt, so he called him a "muckraker."

Jack became a professional speaker in the Joe McCarthy era. He wrote the book, *McCarthy: The Man, the Senator, the Ism*. The Harry Walker Speakers Bureau booked him because of the hot subject matter.

His favorite speaker is John F. Kennedy. Jack told me, "Jack Kennedy was fascinating, a good speaker. He had the ability to be both entertaining and to get down to business. He'd crack a few jokes and then ask, 'Well, Jack, what are you investigating now? What leaks do I have to plug up in Washington?' He'd joke about it.

"President Kennedy had a way that's hard to describe. He had charisma. It was the way he said things, more than what he said... that Camelot aura that he projected, more than what he actually did. Jack Kennedy was a businessman. He had a great ability to concentrate on whatever it was he was doing. In the Oval Office he was a full-time president. When he was out playing touch football, he was a full-time football player. When he was sailing he was a full time sailor."

The ability to focus, to concentrate, is a trait I have found in every great speaker I have chosen for this book. Jack Anderson told me, "Dottie, probably the most dynamic guy I've heard speak is Boris Yeltsin, President of Russia. He has this staccato, machine gun speech. He is bold, brash, forceful. However, Winston Churchill was the most impressive speaker of all. He had a way of expressing himself verbally that was better than most people could write, including myself. It just came right off the top of his head with great drama and flair, without appearing to be dramatic. He was good. I was a very young reporter when Churchill was Prime Minister and Roosevelt was President."

I asked Jack Anderson if he agreed with Aristotle's definition of a great speaker. He thought a moment, then replied, "There is something to what Aristotle says. I think that it's absolutely essential to say what you believe in. Speak your convictions. Stand up. Speak up. When I speak I give them solid credibility."

Lenora Billings-Harris
One of the United States' top black speakers,
internationally famous. "Diversity, the Silent
Revolution"

Lenora Billings-Harris

Here is a great, talented speaker who happens to be female, happens to be black. She speaks about the changing work force in America, calling diversity "The Silent Revolution." Lenora helped manage the largest educational initiative in the automotive industry in her role as regional coordinator for Chrysler's Customer-One program. Lenora helped manage the delivery of culture-change training to sixty thousand people.

She was selected by People to People International to be a delegate to Russia and the Ukraine, to share human resource development work force diversity ideas and techniques with government and industry leaders.

Known as "the marble lady," Lenora says, "Marbles are like people, all pretty much alike. But each unique and different. Diversity is more than just a cultural, gender, or racial issue. When you fail to see the basic differences in behavioral style, values, and beliefs, you overlook the potential of each individual. Women, minorities, seniors, and physically challenged workers are advancing. It's time to go beyond the ideals of equal opportunity and affirmative action."

Typical of Lenora's creativity, she hands out small cards printed with great thoughts. Example: "People need your love the most when they appear to deserve it least." — John Harrigan.

She was inspired by Dr. Layne Longfellow, psychologist, speaker, and seminar leader. Dr. Longfellow was formerly a college vice-president. He joined the Menninger Foundation as director of seminars for executives. His programs include his own piano music and beautiful slides, a combination he calls "lecture theater."

Lenora says, "I first experienced Dr. Longfellow's uniqueness when I heard him deliver an awe-inspiring message about our environment. He used music, lecture, video, and photography. I thought him the professional's professional. My favorite quote from that program was: "As we strive to add years to our lives, let's be sure to add life to our years."

Somers White
Expert in the banking and business world,
author, speaker, famous internationally

Lenora is one of the thousands of great women speakers on the American platform. She makes us proud.

Somers White

When I first met Somers White I stood in awe. He had been one of the youngest bank managers in the country. Under his management, his bank's deposits went from zero to thirty-three million dollars in just eighteen months. He was a state senator from Arizona and president of the Phoenix Society of Financial Analysts. He holds his master's degree from the Harvard Business School. Somers began his business career with the executive training program of the Chase Manhattan Bank.

Here is the kind of brilliant man who does not "suffer fools easily." It took a long time before he became my friend and advisor. To be considered one of his legion of friends is to possess a treasure indeed.

Somers always arrives early for each program. His microphone, props, slides, lighting, air conditioning—every detail of the room is arranged with meticulous care. The true professional. He has spoken in all fifty states and on six continents. My *Sharing Ideas Newsmagazine* elected him to its Speakers Hall of Fame and featured him on the cover as the "consummate professional speaker."

Somers is equally well known as an international consultant. People fly in to his Phoenix office from all over the world to ask his advice and receive his counsel.

He often quotes his father, Paul A. White, who was the speaker who inspired Somers. "Paul White had a strong sense of right and wrong. He had commitment and was always in the pursuit of excellence. He was an avid reader, even when he was eighty years old. Always current and vital with tremendous energy. He had both breadth and depth of information, but if he didn't know, he never hesitated to say he didn't know.

"My father did not like to waste time, money, or any resource. He was willing to practice for every performance. He was always prepared, early, and on time. He was lively, fun, enthusiastic, and interesting, but always more interested in other people. He encouraged me in anything

I did. He almost always responded to my ideas and projects with 'Terrific!'

"He advised me about speaking: 'When talking to the audience, always look at one person at a time and let that person feel like you are really talking to him or her. Pretend there is a piano wire from your eye to that person's eye.'

"Our White family motto is 'Through being wounded, I grow stronger.'"

Paul White's advice about women to his son was: "To her faults be a little blind, to her virtues be a little kind."

Paul told Somers, "Follow the example of your mother and always be kind to the blind, the lame, and the halt."

With a mother and father like those, it is no wonder Somers believes "no success in business will ever make up for a failure at home."

Ken Blanchard
World-famous speaker, coauthor, *One Minute Manager* and *Raving Fans*

Chapter 11

Ken Blanchard

Ken Blanchard is well known as the creator of the *One-Minute Manager,* co-authored with Spencer Johnson. He has now authored a series of One-Minute books that have sold more than seventeen million copies and have been translated into twenty languages. His latest hit book is *Raving Fans,* about customer service.

Few speakers have impacted the day-to-day management of people and companies as Ken has. I think it is his neighborly, humorous style I like so much. His advice is practical, down-home, and full of simple truths that dawn on your mind like bright skies after a dark rain. My reaction to his speaking style is that I like him. Ken awakens me to reach up to my higher potential. A great gift. My favorite management quote by Ken is, "Catch your employees doing something right."

When we interviewed Ken for *Sharing Ideas Newsmagazine,* I asked him which speaker had influenced his life and inspired him most. He said: "Dottie, the greatest speaker I have ever heard or worked with is Dr. Norman Vincent Peale. While we worked together on our book, *The Power of Ethical Management,* I heard Norman speak many times. I was amazed about his tremendous energy in front of the audience. I had heard him speak a number of times when he was in his late eighties. The minute he walks on stage his energy and enthusiasm make him seem forty years younger. I remember him saying, 'Feeling good about yourself is a choice. Every morning you can choose to feel good about yourself or feel bad about yourself. Why would you choose the latter?'

"Dr. Peale is a special gift in my life. I'll never forget a few years ago hearing his sermon at the Crystal Cathedral in Garden Grove, California. Dr. Peale was on Dr. Robert Schuller's board of directors and gave a sermon there at least twice a year. Once Norman got on his feet he

Patricia McCormick
Multiple-Gold-Medal, Olympic
diving champion

completely captivated the audience as he again explained the concept of positive thinking and believing in yourself."

Ken Blanchard maintains a faculty position in leadership at the University of Massachusetts, Amherst, and a visiting lectureship at Cornell University. Ken and his brilliant wife, Marjorie, who is also a speaker, own the Blanchard Training and Development Company. When I asked Ken what makes him feel best about his speaking, books, and other vast works, he replied, "Although I speak on a variety of topics, in almost all aspects of my speeches and supporting materials, I relate back to a few central themes:

- Take the 'b.s.' out of the behavioral sciences.
- Be a conveyor of simple truths.
- Remind people that common sense is often not common practice.

If through my efforts I have helped people, that's reward enough to make me proud and happy."

Ken Blanchard is a man who speaks with the tongues of men and of angels and does so with love overflowing.

Pat McCormick

Winning four Olympic Gold Medals takes a whole lot of "never give up" philosophy. Pat McCormick would have one thousand medals on ribbons around her neck if they were also awarded for hard work and a loving "you can do it" for all those around her.

Jim Murray, Pulitzer Prize-winning syndicated sportswriter, described Pat as "one of those larger than life stars of Olympic history. There are Jesse Owens, Jim Thorpe, Mark Spitz, and Pat McCormick."

I am inspired by her spirit. She told me that being able to make a difference in peoples' lives through inspiration and education are what her life is about. Pat said, "Motivation is similar to fitness. You have to hear good ideas and act on them every day. You can't store motivation. My message is intended to put focus, direction, and hope into peoples lives."

Here are the five basic precepts Pat uses in her speeches and coaching:

Wally Amos
The "cookie man." Famous entrepreneur,
humorous speaker/writer

- Dare to dream.
- Work equals efficiency/effects.
- Don't fear failure, welcome it.
- Surround yourself with greatness.
- Step up to the next challenge.

Pat believes that speaking is like diving. The more you put into it, the more you succeed. Her favorite quote is from another person of great accomplishment, General H. Norman Schwarzkopf, who said that "Leadership demands credibility: Leadership is made of integrity, loyalty, and trust. Competence is important, but without credibility, you have nothing."

Pat's daughter, Kelly McCormick, followed in her mother's footsteps and has become an Olympic champion too. They are the only mother/daughter athletes to achieve Olympic gold medals.

Pat was my young grandson's coach at her diver's youth camp. Our Michael said, "When some of the kids were ready to give up, Pat always took them to one side and gave them the heart to go on. I will never forget her." That's credibility.

Pat told me the speaker who most inspired her is NFL twenty-eight–year football referee, Jim Tunney. Jim uses many quotes. Pat remembers these he gave her: "Every great and commanding moment in the annals of the world is the triumph of some enthusiasm," by Ralph Waldo Emerson. "Life is either a daring adventure, or nothing," by blind and deaf Helen Keller.

Pat is one of my favorites because she is a good friend to all those who know her. She reminds me of the explanation of championship given by another Olympic star: "It takes more than athletic skills. If you're not strong in the head, you don't have a chance."

Pat McCormick is also very strong in the heart.

Wally Amos

Before I ever heard Wally Amos speak, I visualized him as a tough New York publicity man, because that was his vocation. He worked for the William Morris Agency and later had his own personal management business for music and entertainment stars such as Simon and Garfunkel and the Temptations.

Wally doesn't fit the stereotype I had of him at all! He is funny, charming, spiritual, plays a kazoo on stage, and wears his famous Hawaiian hat in a jaunty, happy way.

Wally apprenticed as a teenager at a New York trade school and worked as a cook. Everyone thinks of him as the cookie man, so some of the stories he tells on stage are about how he opened his first shop. His cookies were so popular he had to personally keep baking all night to keep up with the demand, like the "sorcerer's apprentice."

He is the American spokesman for the Literacy Volunteers of America and has been inducted into the Babson College Academy of Distinguished Entrepreneurs.

One day when Wally visited our Walters International Speakers Bureau here in Glendora, California, I asked about his world famous cookie recipe. "Was it your grandmother's?"

He told me it was his Aunty Della who first made chocolate chip cookies for him.

"Then it was her recipe you used?"

"Oh, no, Dottie. I just used the recipe on the Toll House chocolate chip package."

What a lesson! Millions of us have used that same recipe. It took a genius of promotion to build a giant business based on it.

Wally reminds me of another unusual man, George Washington Carver, the great inventor, who said: "When you can do the common things in life in an uncommon way, you will command the attention of the world."

It was on that same visit here that our family invited Wally to go with us to our favorite local restaurant for dinner. He ran to his car first and brought with him a large bag. I wondered what was in it.

As the maitre'd seated us, Wally reached into the bag and held out his business card to the man. Attached to the bottom of the card was a little sealed plastic bag with a chocolate chip cookie in it.

The maitre'd was busy. He hardly looked at the card until he walked away from our table. I saw him stop, read it, and do a double-take toward us. Then he ran with it toward the bar.

What a sensation that card and cookie made! The customers passed it up and down the bar, examined it, and pointed to us. Some said, "It can't be HIM!" They nabbed one of the bus boys and made him come over to our table.

He stood by Wally, looking embarrassed. "Would you like one of my cookies, son?" Wally grinned. "Oh, yes, sir!" the boy gasped. He took his treasure and began showing it to the people at the next table, then ran out to the kitchen.

Slowly, those folks at the next table arose and surrounded Wally. All were given cards, cookies, and dazzling smiles. Then the table on the other side stood up and got in line to speak to Wally. They were followed by the customers at the bar and the bartenders. The waitresses came up, the rest of the customers, and, finally, the cooks and dishwashers from the kitchen—until Wally's big bag was empty.

He had never moved. He drew all those people to him like a magnet! Later I asked him, "How many cookies do you give out a day, a week, a month? What does this promotion cost?"

"Oh, I don't know, Dottie," he smiled. "I don't keep track of things like that. You see, I just keep planting seeds."

Wally has a new business now, "The Uncle Noname Cookie Company." On his letterhead are the words, "Turn lemons into lemonade. —Wally Amos, Nephew."

One of Wally's favorite quotes is by Sal Sperlinsa who wrote: "Give the world the best you've got and you will get kicked in the teeth. Give the world the best you've got anyway."

Patricia Fripp

The first time I heard Patricia Fripp, I was intrigued by her clipped Cockney English accent, strong voice, and the size of the spirit in her petite body.

She told the story of how she became the best barber she could be by practicing longer, working harder, and

Patricia Fripp
Past president, National Speakers Association,
international speaker on time management and
"Take Charge of Your Life"

giving her very best effort to every customer. She emigrated to the United States with only a pair of barber shears and fifty dollars in her purse. Pat worked in the financial district of San Francisco and was so entertaining and fun, her customers asked her to come and speak for their service clubs. Pat began her speaking career as I did, speaking free for the wonderful members of the Kiwanis and Rotary, and giving out information about her business.

Pat is an avid reader, listener, and attender of seminars. You see her always in the front row, taking notes, learning from every speaker.

She says, "I have a lot of energy. The biggest thing I had to learn was how to focus it. A lot of people ask you to run this, be on this board, do this or that. I had to learn to say no, to focus on my priorities. I believe you can say no but still support people. I had my hair styling business in the same building as the chamber of commerce. One of my friends on their staff asked if I would run a monthly luncheon for their volunteers. I had to say no because I travel too much. However, I told them, "Once a year I'll give you a free speech to rev up your team.""

Pat is a time-management expert. I asked her how she handles the bane of all people of accomplishment—interruptions.

She replied, "On the phone, learn how to get off before you get on. I say: "Got your message, what can I do for you?"

They say, "How are you, Patricia?"

"Busy, what can I do for you?"

"I'll call you later."

"I'm busy later. What can I do for you now? I have just five minutes."

Get to the point. Other people are busy. If you have a reputation that when you call someone you will hold them up for ten minutes, then they are under pressure. Get respect for other people's time."

Patricia Fripp is very popular with speakers bureaus because she goes all out to be cooperative, helpful, and to deliver a wonderful performance every time, a team player. She reminds me of this quote by David Starr

Dewitt Jones
National Geographic photographer, inspirational
speaker on focus on life

Johnson: "The world stands aside to let those pass who know where they are going."

Dewitt Jones

The great photographer, Dewitt Jones reminds me of this quote about "seeing," by William Blake: "To see a world in a grain of sand and a heaven in a wildflower, hold infinity in the palm of your hand and eternity in an hour."

Dewitt is an award-winning National Geographic photographer who explores the fundamentals of creativity in his energizing programs. Using his own breath-taking photography as examples, he awakens within us our own powerful creative potential. I love the quote he uses by Dag Hammarskjold of the United Nations. "Then a tree becomes a mystery, a cloud, a revelation, each human a cosmos of whose riches we can only catch glimpses."

Dewitt tells the story of a little boy who followed him one day as he set up his cameras for a shoot. The child had a toy camera made of plastic in garish comic-style colors. The boy watched his every move with rapt attention. He mimicked the great photographer, pretended to set his camera with great care, and sighted off through it into the distance.

Dewitt was amused and flattered. Finally the little boy asked if he might ask him an important question. Thinking of this great opportunity to teach the younger generation, Dewitt smiled and said, "Of course."

"What flavor juice is in your camera?" the little guy asked.

Dewitt is full of surprises, beauty, and art. He is a motion picture director who had two films nominated for Academy Awards before he was thirty. For fifteen years National Geographic sent him all over the globe, earning him a reputation as an exceptional photojournalist. He is well known as a creative corporate marketing photographer and has written seven books.

I love his open, relaxed style which is the opposite of arrogance. He shows his audience a large color photograph, a panorama. Then he takes us with his artist's eyes to focus in on the most beautiful thing of all, perhaps a bird drinking from a tiny stream with a rainbow of color breaking in the water's mist. His lesson is to focus. Breathtaking.

Dewitt told me that he listened to the tapes of many speakers when he began. He said, "I sadly found many who were slick, excessively mental, or both. I wondered if speaking was not for me.

"Then I attended a presentation by Rosita Perez. She stood there with her guitar and smile and simply opened her heart. She shared it all, gifts, flaws, highs, lows— everything that makes her who she is. She spoke with humor, compassion, and joy. She sang the song of her life that day, until I couldn't help but sing my own. She has been my inspiration ever since." Dewitt said this favorite quote by Rosita made his own heart sing, "In the chorus of life, the music is you."

Another of Dewitt's favorite quotes is by the great naturalist, John Muir. "I have discovered that I also live in 'creation's dawn'. The morning stars still sing together, and the world, not yet half made, becomes more beautiful every day."

As I traveled on a plane recently, I had the good fortune to sit opposite Dewitt. He handed me a gift across the aisle. A little plastic juice camera with a personal message to me written on it. He said, "Dottie, remember to focus." I know what flavor mine is: Inspiring.

Rosita Perez
Sizzling American-Latin speaker/writer,
musician, inspirer

Chapter 12

Rosita Perez

Rosita Perez is an inspiration to many in the speaking world. Her philosophy is, "You and I have a choice. Either we lament all the high notes we can't or won't hit, or we leave those to Pavarotti and get on with the rest of our songs."

I especially enjoy her programs when she adds music, making her guitar pick up the beat until the entire audience participates with joy. Her music is life-transforming. I know she has encouraged many to commit to making their own kind of music.

Rosita told me that the greatest speaker she ever heard was Dr. Leo Buscaglia. She saw him on tape in a college classroom. He had that magic quality that great speakers often have: He made her feel he was speaking only to her.

"Leo Buscaglia had removed his jacket and spoke in shirt-sleeves," Rosita said. "He perspired. He wiped his brow. He spoke of 'Mama' and eating polenta as a kid. His father asked them around the dining room table each night, 'What did you learn today?' In that hour, my life was transformed. It was only then that I understood the power of the spoken word when delivered with conviction and passion, mixed with humor and love. Above all, love.

"Until that day, I had assumed that only perfect media personalities were listened to on the platform. With Dr. Buscaglia's tape I finally comprehended that McLuhan was right: 'The medium *is* the message.' I had heard it before, but had not understood until that moment. It was life-transforming."

Rosita holds her degree in social work. She is the former associate director of the Mental Health Association of Miami, Florida. She is an authority on the use of music for other than entertainment—yet she does not read a note of music. She is a great natural talent.

She says the quote she likes most by a speaker is this one: "The only problem with climbing the ladder of

Chris Hegarty
Top U.S. business speaker/author

success too furiously is that you must be careful that when you reach the top, you don't look down and realize your ladder is leaning against the wrong building!"

Chris Hegarty

Chris Hegarty is a speaker who makes you *think*. The first time I heard him he told his audience, "It is easier to make excuses for not thinking by using cliches, e.g. 'When in Rome, do as Romans do.' It didn't work for them! Their life expectancy was twenty-two years. *Think!* Don't respond with cliches. Risk saying something that is really you."

Chris is a powerful speaker who has presented to more than four hundred of the Fortune 500 companies, as well as many other organizations in twenty-seven countries. While he has many topics, I especially like his program on the consistently exceptional leader. Chris believes leadership is a process that can be learned. His five precepts of getting high levels of performance from people have helped me many times in my companies. They are: selecting, training, organizing, communicating with, and keeping good people.

I asked Chris about the great speaker who inspired him. He replied: "It was Earl Nightingale. I asked for the opportunity to introduce Earl on six occasions when we spoke at rallies together. On one occasion I got stuck in a blizzard for three days because of waiting to introduce him. (It was worth it!) Each time I introduced him, Earl got a standing ovation as he came out on stage, and again when he finished. This was my introduction: 'Ladies and Gentlemen, we have honored warriors who have fought for us on the battlefield, we have honored warriors who have fought for us to master technology. When it comes time to honor the warriors who are involved in the most important war of all—the war against our own ignorance, one name will always appear at the top of the list. He is your next speaker, Ladies and Gentlemen. Please welcome Earl Nightingale!'

"Frankly, I still get a little caught up when I think about him. He was a great human being. I learned much from

Maxine McIntyre Hammond
Brilliant international speaker, past national
board member, National Speakers Association

him. My favorite Nightingale quote: 'Select what you think about with great care. It will almost certainly happen!'"

Maxine McIntyre Hammond

Maxine is an eloquent speaker. She is a beautifully dressed, elegant, poised woman who has spoken in twenty-seven countries of the world. Her husband, John Hammond, is an impresario who books many famous speakers such as Brian Tracy, Zig Ziglar, and Og Mandino.

The first time I heard Maxine tell her own story I was shocked. She was the sixth of eleven children. The family lived in a three-room shack in New Mexico, raising chickens, grain, a garden, and a few cows for butter and cream which they sold to buy staples. Their clothes were made from feed sacks. The children were often hungry. They moved to California when drought hit their area.

"Those who have read John Steinbeck's *Grapes of Wrath* have a perfect picture of us," Maxine told her audience. "My mother took seven of us children in our old car, pulling all our worldly goods behind us in a homemade trailer. We threw mattresses on the desert at night and used streams to bathe. One of my big brothers drove back later for the rest of the family.

"No one would rent us a place to stay in Sacramento. My Aunt and Uncle persuaded a dairy farm to let us clean out their chicken coop to sleep in. We picked crops and gradually got all of us in school. By eighteen, I married and had my first baby. I helped my husband through school to become a doctor, but after our sixth child was born, he left us. Then, with the help of my children I went back to school and earned three college degrees."

Maxine spoke one day at the American River College, and upon glancing out the window realized she was looking down at the broken weather vane atop that same old chicken coop her family slept in when they first arrived in Sacramento! Everyone in the audience had tears in their eyes, realizing what a great spirit she has. Today's Cinderella, who had a dream, six kids, and no husband to help her.

John Patrick Dolan
Attorney at law, delightful Irish-American
speaker, author, *Negotiate Like a Pro*

Maxine's favorite speaker is Tom Sullivan, who, though blind, plays the piano and sings as part of his program. "He spoke with so much confidence and love for his audience," she says. "All I have to do is close my eyes and see him, and I am renewed."

The quote she was influenced by was the same one by Bill Gove which influenced our teenaged son to become an attorney. "You are not responsible *for* the people in your audience. You are responsible *to* them. Give them the very best you can, every time."

Maxine says, "Bill's words had such an impact on me because many of my audiences were law enforcement officers. Some fell asleep or walked out for a few minutes. I was hurt, worried I wasn't doing my job.

"Then I learned that many officers had worked a double shift. Some had rushed children to the hospital the night before. They slipped out to call and check on how those children were doing. None of their actions had anything to do with me. Bill Gove's words proved to be true blue."

John Patrick Dolan

John has a charming Irish personality that beguiles everyone he meets. He has spoken in many countries of the world. Negotiation is one of his great topics. He is the author of the famous Putnam book, *Negotiate Like the Pros*. John set up the first dispute-resolution service for speakers and speakers bureaus and has been of excellent service to many in the industry. I love the quote John uses to close each program:

> *"May the road rise to meet you.*
> *May the sun shine warm on your face.*
> *May the wind always be at your back.*
> *May the rain fall softly on your fields.*
> *And until we meet again,*
> *May the good Lord hold you*
> *in the palm of His hand."*

Being a professional practicing attorney, it is not surprising that John was inspired first by the brilliant

James Hennig
Past president, National Speakers Association,
famous business speaker

lawyer, F. Lee Bailey. John says: "I actually had legal courtroom experience with F. Lee Bailey. He inspired me as a trial lawyer. Trial lawyering is really just a special kind of speaking with small audiences of about twelve and judges. I can tell you that I have never seen anyone be so intense or so charismatic, or so focused on the important issues, as F. Lee Bailey. In the trial we had together his cross-examination was a model of what good lawyers should do in court to make sure that the truth comes out, and that innocent people were not convicted wrongly. Lee had a tremendous influence over me.

"The most captivating general-subject speaker I ever heard is Carl Hammerschlag. I'll never forget the first time I heard him. I have pretty high standards, and if the truth were known, I do not recognize too many good speakers in the entire country. There are a lot of adequate ones who do a good job, but the kind who really grab your attention and won't let you go are rare. Carl is one of these. He told a story from his book, *The Theft of the Spirit,* which knocked me off my chair. The way he used his voice and manipulated the language, combined with his storytelling techniques, were overwhelming, mind-grabbing, captivating."

John Patrick Dolan told me, "Dottie, Cavett Robert said this about how to approach your audience. It has stuck in my mind for every performance. 'They don't care how much you know, until they know how much you care.'"

"I have taken Cavett's words to heart. If we are to be successful as speakers, we need to be very concerned about what happens from the audience's point of view. We must show them we are concerned, caring, and interested in their getting the ideas we convey."

It is obvious to me that the good Lord holds John Patrick Dolan in the hollow of His hand.

James F. Hennig

Jim Hennig is the kind of man everyone calls friend. He is a businessman, educator, author, athlete (member of the University of Wisconsin Big Ten Championship

Ed Foreman

Earlene Vining
Top international business speaking team

Football Team), and a pilot. Jim is an outstanding family man with a high sense of integrity. I like his energy and enthusiasm. He is the kind of man we like the world to believe is typical of the United States. He has taught at Purdue University and served as president of the National Speakers Association.

The speaker who first inspired Jim Hennig is W. Clement Stone. Jim relates: "I have not had the privilege of hearing Mr. Stone in person, but have listened so much to recordings of presentations he has made. I'm a tape junkie and listen to many, many tapes, because I appreciate the power of spaced repetition to help impress those great ideas on my mind.

"The quotation which Mr. Stone made in his speech which had the most lasting influence on my life is this: 'There is very little difference between people, but that little difference makes a great difference.'

"How true that statement is. Whenever I meet people in my travels and in my audience who have excelled greatly and reached the top of their profession, I realize there is very little difference between them and those who are at the average level. But that little difference makes a big difference. So I realize with every presentation I make that participants need not walk away with fifty or one hundred new ideas, their lives may be changed with two or three great ones. That little difference makes all the difference."

Jim Hennig reminds me of a favorite quote by Jim Rohn: "If you just communicate you can get by. But if you skillfully communicate, you can work miracles."

Ed Foreman and Earlene Vining

When I attended the Successful Life seminar which Ed and Earlene present, I was impressed by the kind of people who attended—engineers, scientists, executives, CEOs. All were fascinated, leaning forward in their chairs, taking notes as Ed and Earlene presented a fast-paced set of events which inspired, taught, and trained all of us who were fortunate enough to be there.

Earlene told the story of wanting a "store-bought" dress so badly when she was a little girl, she clipped a picture from the mail order catalog and tacked it up by her bed. Her mama made her dresses from feed sacks.

When her birthday came, her mama gave her a package wrapped with tissue and tied with a ribbon. Earlene burst into tears when she opened it, because she could see the material had come from another feed sack.

"You hush your tears, Earlene!" her mother said. "This is no dress. It's a great big double-lined sack with a strap to hang over your shoulder so you can go out with the big kids and pick cotton. With this tool you can work and earn your own money. And anyone who can do that, can have any dress in the world that she wants!" What a profound truth. What a great woman.

Earlene has spoken in many countries all over the world. She always wears beautiful clothes. I think of her Mama each time I see her perform. How proud she must be. Earlene told me that Ed Foreman has been her ongoing speaking inspiration because he is committed to excellence.

"As a business associate and coach, Ed has taught me not only the joy of speaking, but the skills and fundamentals to attract speaking engagements. It is always exciting to have the opportunity to thank him personally and publicly."

I understand how Earlene feels. Ed Foreman has always been a great friend and mentor to me too. What a marvelous man. Ed made his first million by the time he was twenty-six. He was elected to Congress at the age of twenty-eight. He is the only person in this century to have been elected to the U.S. Congress from two different states (Texas and New Mexico). He has enjoyed a close working relationship with five U.S. presidents. Ed is president of Executive Development Systems of Dallas. You may have seen him on CBS News' "60 Minutes."

Ed said to me, "Will Rogers said, 'I never met a man I didn't like.' Well, I never met or listened to a speaker from whom I didn't learn something useful. I make it a regular practice, when I am not speaking or conducting seminars, to attend programs conducted by others. I go to listen, learn, and enjoy. Sometimes I learn and enjoy more than at other times, but there's always a lesson. Even if it's how *not* to do something!

"One of my original mentors was Dr. Kenneth McFarland, a master storyteller. He used vivid personal examples to drive home important lessons. He was an orator who practiced what he preached. He varied his speed, modulated his voice, and captured the audience with intense feeling and sincerity.

"Dale Carnegie was another loved and appreciated mentor who taught me that a good thirty-minute speech was simply ten or twelve two-minute stories laced together with brief key lessons or points. He lived and breathed enthusiasm, vibrancy, and vitality.

"Earl Nightingale held my attention by his impassioned, persuasive eloquence. Jose Silva helped me to better understand the power of the utilization of my subconscious mind. Cavett Robert and Zig Ziglar demonstrated the value of body language, stage performance, movement with feeling, and conviction.

"Florence Littauer reminded me—no—made me understand, that everyone is different and will not respond in the same way. Even though some in the audience may appear disinterested, aloof, or enthusiastic, it is just a personality difference, not a personal rejection.

"Earlene Vining taught me to lighten up. She impressed upon me the importance of thinking, acting, and looking like a winner.

"Dr. Norman Vincent Peale taught me the power of feeling love and appreciation for every member of my audience, to be tolerant, kinder, and more understanding of everyone.

"Each one of these great speakers, friends, and mentors taught me one of the most important lessons for any speaker. They all walk their talk. They speak what they live, and they live what they speak."

I love Ed's use of a quote from another favorite of mine, Dr. Viktor Frankl, who was held as a Nazi prisoner at Auschwitz during World War II. "We had to teach the despairing men that it did not really matter what we expected from life, but rather what life expected from us."

William F. Buckley, Jr.
Multi-talented speaker/author, TV host,
magazine publisher/editor

Chapter 13

William F. Buckley, Jr.

Perhaps you have heard William F. Buckley as he hosts his "Firing Line" television show, or perhaps you are one of the lucky ones who have heard him speak in person in auditoriums all over the world.

The first thing I noticed about him was the flash of brilliance in his eyes. They are like beacons signaling intelligence and enthusiasm.

William F. Buckley, Jr., graduated with honors from Yale University. He is an author, presidential advisor, international columnist, politician, publisher, adventurer, editor, philosopher, and TV personality. He founded and is editor of the conservative journal, *The National Review*.

He writes a column, "On the Right," which appears three times a week in over three hundred major American newspapers and dozens of other publications throughout the world. His "Firing Line" TV show won an Emmy Award. He received the TV Guide Award for best television interviewer.

William F. Buckley, Jr. has been a presidential appointee to the U.S. Information Agency, the United Nations, and the National Security Council. He has made three transoceanic sailing voyages, journeyed to the South Pole, and is the author of several best-selling travel books. His many other books have a tremendous range—from novels to children's stories, politics, and philosophy. His mystery book, *Stained Glass*, won the American Book Award for Best Mystery.

He has been awarded over thirty-five honorary doctorates as well as the International Platform Association's Ralph Waldo Emerson Award. Here is an American treasure. We chose him as our Consummate Speaker of the Year for our *Sharing Ideas Newsmagazine*.

It was an immense thrill for me to interview William F. Buckley, Jr., for our newsmagazine. With a record like his, my first question was, "Who inspired you?"

Mr. Buckley replied, "My father was scornful of bad reasoning, and I suppose I inherited that trait. The result is that I am always consciously or subconsciously ferreting out bad logic or inconsistencies."

I asked how he began speaking.

"I attended a boarding school in Millbrook, New York, whose founder required every single school boy to give a speech to the entire assembly once a year. It was a horrifying experience, but it taught us all to speak publicly. Later, I joined the debating team.

"In the army I was an infantry basic training instructor, which required me to lecture to platoons and even companies at age nineteen. At Yale, I again joined the debate team."

Then I asked Mr. Buckley, "What was the most difficult audience you ever encountered?"

He answered, "Probably the most difficult was the student body of American University in 1969, soon after the Cambodian incursion. It was an outdoor meeting in the spring. The hosts made the mistake of lowering the lighting when I began speaking.

"A Black Panther group began heckling. The device was interesting and effective: They would laugh without stopping anytime I spoke anything faintly risible. When I made a point—any point—they would applaud and continue applauding.

"After fifteen minutes I stopped and said this was not what I came to the university for. There ensued a threatened brawl between the students who wanted to hear me and the disrupters.

"The dean of the law school pleaded with me to continue: I did and left. That is the only interruption I've ever had."

Then I asked Mr. Buckley which of his many, many awards was closest to his heart. He replied, "I wouldn't disguise that I am proudest of the United States Medal of Freedom. I fancied myself as a young man involved in a fight for freedom. It was gratifying to receive acknowledgement at that level in company with so many people so much more deserving than I."

As you can see by his comments, Mr. Buckley is brilliant, human, and humble.

Our good friend Somers White says about this great speaker: "At first William F. Buckley, Jr., appears slow and methodical. Then he is at the jugular vein. Seeing him work is like watching a champion chess player who suddenly calls 'checkmate!' He is a master."

Jeff Dewar

Jeff Dewar comes from a family long associated with the word quality. His dad, Don Dewar, is one of the founders of the internationally famous QCI Institute that also publishes *The Quality Digest*. Jeff is a polished, smooth professional whose enthusiasm is contagious, one who is always a pleasure to work with. He gives much more than is expected and receives rave reviews from every organization that books him.

Jeff presents his programs in South America, Europe, Africa, and North America, and is equally popular in all of these diverse places. He is that rare speaker who can deliver high-tech knowledge with charm and humor.

We asked Jeff which speaker had inspired him most. He said pilot Dave Carey, the great Vietnam War hero, is high on his list. Dave Carey, one of the great speakers in this book, was incarcerated in Vietnam for five long years. Here is the part of Dave's message which touched Jeff's heart and "sent shivers of proud self-reliance down my spine:

"When it comes to taking care of yourself, take charge. Nobody can do it, will do it, wants to do it, or knows how to do it."

Here are Jeff Dewar's favorite quotes about speaking:

Mark Twain: "It's not what you don't know that gets you into trouble, it's what you know for sure that ain't so."

Lilly Walters: "Nervous? Stop thinking about yourself and start thinking about your audience. Then go out and enjoy yourself and the audience will enjoy you!"

Dottie Walters: "Think of each person in your audience as a little Oliver Twist, with that empty bowl raised up in his two small hands, his eyes asking for more. You are

Jeff Dewar
International Total Quality expert

the one who will fill their bowls with the nourishment of your knowledge."

Larry King: "You can always spot pure talent—they are the people who are doing what they do simply for themselves—and not worrying about what others will think."

Jeff says, "I know that Larry King's quote seems a bit in contradiction with Lilly's and Dottie's, but I see them as mutually supportive. I think a speaker can do what they love to do in the spirit of empathy."

Hope Mihalap

Hope Mihalap has to have one of the hardest names to pronounce of all the great speakers I have ever met. I finally mastered it when I realized the first syllable is *Mi*, then *hal*, then *ap*. Synonymous to me with laughing uproariously. She is one of the funniest women speakers I have ever had the pleasure to hear. She is a master of dialects and is the character voice behind hundreds of radio and TV commercials.

The titles of her programs bring a grin before you are seated. One of her program titles, "Swimming Through the Melting Pot" is a typical hilarious zinger.

Hope is a descendant of the first Greek family to settle in Virginia and is married to a Russian-born professor. When she tells the story of her Greek grandmother who only learned one English word in her entire life, you expect something deeply cultural and profound. Then Hope explodes that one English word—"EAT!"

I thought the audience would never quiet down. No matter what nationality our grandmothers were, they all said the same thing to us.

Hope is a very cultured, educated lady, a graduate of Vassar College, who with her husband speaks seven languages. She served as the private secretary to Sir Rudolf Bing, head of the Metropolitan Opera. She is the recipient of awards from the National Speakers Association and of the Mark Twain Award for Humor awarded by the International Platform Association. Past recipients of the

Hope Mihalap
Top multi-accent, hilarious humorist

Mark Twain Award are Bob Hope, Danny Kaye, Phyllis Diller, Mark Russell, and Erma Bombeck.

Hope told us that the first great speaker she ever heard and the one who influenced her most was her father, Chris P. Christopoulos, a native of Cyprus and a naturalized American citizen.

Hope told me, "My father had a natural gift for oratory and for relating humorous anecdotes. When he spoke at local church or political events, he mesmerized the audience by his delivery and choice of words. His first language was Greek. In Greek oratory he had no peers. In English his vocabulary was less elegant, but he had a natural sense of timing and dramatic wit."

Two American speakers who have inspired Hope are Dorothy DeBolt and Gerald Coffee. "These two professionals bring warmth, humor, a sense of love, and a total lack of pretension to their presentations. They have inspired me to keep foremost in my mind a sense of affection for my audience," she explains.

Delightful Hope shared with us her two favorite quotes: "The reports of my death have been greatly exaggerated," by Mark Twain.

"We have met the enemy and he is us!" Walt Kelly, cartoonist/author of "Pogo."

Hope says: "While these are by no means the cleverest things these men ever said, they are memorable to me because I read them at an early age. Suddenly I understood the unique spark of humor behind them. Great humor has an element of the unexpected in it, of strange and witty contrast.

"To my young eyes, these quotes alerted me to the possibility of saying unusual, clever things myself. I have been impressed by many others, in particular some of the great ones of Martin Luther King and the benevolent wisdom of Will Rogers."

Terry Paulson

From the moment Terry Paulson steps out on the stage, you realize he is full of twinkling fun. He presents his profound wisdom in a uniquely entertaining and witty

Terry Paulson
Board of Directors, NSA, humorous
business speaker

style. No wonder he has been called "the Will Rogers of management consultants," by *Business Digest* magazine.

Terry is a licensed psychologist, author, and editor of *Management Dialogue* newsletter. He is the host and interviewer for the ECI business television series, "Quality From the Human Side," and is the author of several excellent business books including *They Shoot Managers, Don't They?*

Terry told us his favorite quote is from a famous speaker who had quite an impact on the world. The prophet Isaiah: "Those who hope in the Lord will renew their strength. They will soar on the wings of eagles." (Isaiah 40:31).

Terry told us, "That statement has centered my message and my strength in a very strong foundation. I believe life is meant to be lived in faith. The result is a life of joy."

He continued, "My first boss, Jack Nichols, believed in me, listened to me, and helped me develop when I was seventeen. He taught me this quote: 'Every person I work with knows something better than me. My job is to listen long enough to find it and use it.' This quote helps me focus on the value of every member of my audience. I have something to share with them, but I respect them and what each has to offer."

Terry remembers that Cavett Robert said something that hit a chord in his heart. Several of the great speakers in this book have cherished this beautiful quote: "They don't care how much you know, until they know how much you care."

Terry says, "That is my lifeline. Before I speak I say a prayer. 'Help me not just to shine, but to serve.' This prayer dissolves fear and performance anxiety, and connnects me with why I do what I do."

The first speaker who opened Terry's mind to the possibility of his own speaking was Leo Buscaglia. He explains, "I first experienced Leo on a PBS special. He captured, nurtured, and touched the audience. He radiated his message and was not afraid to break all the rules of formal speaking. He let his 'child' and loving acceptance reach everyone. His message of hope and acceptance didn't come from a text or from studies or statistics, but from the heart.

W Mitchell

World-famous wheelchair speaker, who rose
above two physical disasters. Consultant,
brilliant international speaker

"Leo taught me an important lesson. Let your natural speaking style emerge. When audiences know you are authentic, that you have done your homework to prepare a message worth hearing and are there to serve them, you can't do anything wrong.

"They take you in their arms, they smile with their very being, they hug you and your message. Leo hugged them back! He is my speaking hero. I go to him in my mind every time I need a lift."

W Mitchell

The first time I saw W Mitchell I, like most people, was shocked at his physical appearance. He was terribly burned in a flaming motorcycle accident which took his fingers, his face, and nearly his life. He has suffered many operations and skin grafts. Then he was paralyzed from the waist down in a plane crash. My heart was full of pity and my eyes filled with tears as I looked at him. Then I heard his great voice.

W Mitchell has a deep, strong, moving voice that lifts you right out of your chair. His keen mind is electric with ideas. Audiences adore him and give him ovation after ovation. He talks about the wonderful things in his life and how he uses them.

He is known as "the man who would not be defeated" (which is the title of his great WRS book). When you hear him talk about what you *do* with what you have being what matters, you realize he is one of the wisest, bravest men you have ever known.

Listening to Mitchell is a life-changing experience. You cannot help but be inspired to win every battle, overcome all challenges, and "screw your courage to the sticking place," as Will Shakespeare advises.

Mitchell has been called upon to meet with Presidents and cabinet members, to testify before numerous congressional hearings, and to speak all over the world to large companies, associations, and universities, including Harvard, Stanford, and the University of California at Berkeley.

Many speakers have written about him, including Anthony Robbins in his *Unlimited Power* and *Awaken the Giant Within*. Award-winning travel and naturalist writer Michael Frome devoted a whole chapter in his *Promised Land* to Mitchell's courageous attitude and inspiration.

When I asked this great master speaker which speaker had inspired him most he told me: "I've heard lots of speakers. I was very impressed with Paul Harvey and his news broadcast when I was a young high school student. Later on I became aware of another great speaker who was a radio personality, Earl Nightingale. However, the speaker who inspired me most is Ken Blanchard. His quote, "Good guys may appear to come in last, but they're really in a different race," is especially memorable. I was on a program with Ken at the Windstar Foundation before I became a professional speaker."

Mitchell continued, "I wouldn't classify Ken Blanchard as the person possessing the greatest platform skills. In fact, his eye contact, rapport-building skills with an audience, and a variety of other techniques are not those that you would expect to be taught in 'speaker school.' Ken Blanchard speaks from the heart, speaks a message in a conversational, almost lackadaisical manner. He wanders through his talks telling stories, giving insights, almost as if he were just plucked from the audience and asked to say a few words about nothing in particular.

"And yet, as you sit there listening, you realize Ken's messages are profound. The information he imparts and the way he imparts it sneaks up on you and travels deep into your consciousness, before you even know it. I am impressed with Ken Blanchard, because when he speaks to audiences, they realize they are not getting a performance, they are getting instead a wonderful opportunity to have a talk with someone who has thought a lot about the important issues beyond dollars and cents."

And I am completely impressed with W Mitchell, who is the embodiment of the great unbeatable human spirit. He often uses this quote in his programs: "In the midst of winter, I finally learned there was in me an invincible summer." —Albert Camus.

Tom Hopkins
America's Top Sales Trainer, author,
international speaker

Chapter 14

Tom Hopkins

Not only is Tom Hopkins one of the best sales speakers I have had the pleasure of hearing, he is known as the world's number one sales trainer. Tom told me it was the media that added up the number of people he had trained and dubbed him number one. No wonder! To date he has trained well over two million salespeople.

I have found him a prince to work with. His staff is courteous and helpful, and they certainly practice all the great principles Tom teaches. His style is bright, up, with an almost boyish enthusiasm and true pleasure in the success of others. When I asked Tom which speaker had first inspired him, this is the story he told me:

"When I first got into selling, I had hard times. The biggest frustration I had was not knowing where to turn for help. Or, maybe it was not getting the help I really needed when I turned to my manager or other salespeople.

"However, I was very fortunate to find people to learn from who had a powerful impact on my career. Without them I might have given up. Once I stopped trying sales and committed myself to becoming a student of selling, things started getting better for me careerwise, and of course, financially as well.

"It was after I had had some success that I was fortunate to hear a speaker whose message hit me like a ton of bricks. At his program, Jim Rohn was able to help me crystallize in my mind why I needed to continue to study and learn human emotions and how to apply that knowledge to sales.

"Jim Rohn also made me realize how important it was to study and learn in other areas that affected my life. His ideas profoundly affected my financial situation, my future goals, physical health and mental well-being.

"His program made such a difference in my life that to this day I am a dedicated Jim Rohn student. I was amazed at how easily I began to learn once it was a matter of my choice. It wasn't anything like being in a formal education program where I had to talk myself into studying. What a wonderful gift I received the day I sat in Jim Rohn's audience."

Jim Rohn is one of my favorites too. I shared one of my favorite Jim Rohn quotes with Tom Hopkins:

"Learning is the beginning of wealth.

Learning is the beginning of health.

Learning is the beginning of spirituality.

Searching and learning is where the miracle process all begins.

Formal education will make you a living;

Self-education will make you a fortune."

Another great influence in Tom Hopkins' life began the day he enrolled in a seminar conducted by the late, great, J. Douglas Edwards, then known as the "father of American selling." Here is how Tom told me the story:

"At that J. Douglas Edwards' program, I was challenged, instructed, and inspired to learn over sixty closing techniques.

"Doug was a strict taskmaster. He expected us to work hard and excel in his course. After all, our livelihoods depended on our ability to sell. It was incredulous to him that any of the students in his course might not take the training seriously, or that they would do anything but their best.

"I believe he understood salespeople better than most trainers. He included competition in his course for salespeople. He had awards and trophies sitting there in the front of the room. He talked about them like they were made of solid gold. He created in me the burning desire to take home the first-place trophy for that class.

"My life changed in the field of selling because of that three-day Edwards' training session. Yes, I did win that trophy. I slept less than six hours during those three days. I refused to let myself disappoint this wonderful man who knew the greatness that was in me.

"He inspired me beyond my wildest dreams, then showed me how to reach those dreams. I'll never forget the impact of his message. It was priceless.

"I have told this story throughout the world, giving credit for much of my success to Doug. He was the guru of how-to sales training, the only one in the fifties, sixties, and seventies who taught the actual art of closing the sale. As I travel around the country and analyze the training programs for many of the major Fortune 500 companies, I am amazed to see the influence of J. Douglas Edwards' message in their current training programs.

"The message may still be there, but unfortunately the inspiring influence of the man has passed. I will always remember the level of confidence Doug had in me and the pride in his eyes when he saw my dreams to become a speaker realized."

Over two million salespeople are grateful that Tom Hopkins picked up the torch when it was passed to him by the great J. Douglas Edwards.

Joe J. Charbonneau

The first time you meet Joe Charbonneau, you know instantly that you have found a friend. He is hearty and fun, and full of positive, shining ideas.

When business hit a slump, Joe organized seminars for small associations, giving training to their members and work to many speakers who became part of his team on the extremely successful project. When his dear wife became ill with multiple sclerosis, Joe bought a beautiful big motor home so that he could take her with him when he speaks. They go on weekend jaunts to lakes and beautiful places where she can rest and he can work with his computer and printer.

I know him well and have never spoken to him that he has not cheered me and encouraged me, as I know he does to all who are lucky enough to work with him. When I asked Joe who were the speakers who inspired him most, this is what he told me:

"The first great speaker I heard was Bob Richards, the Olympic decathlon champion. I heard him at the Junior

Joe Charbonneau
Board of Directors, NSA, U.S. expert in Sales and
Customer Service, author/speaker

Olympics in St. Paul, Minnesota. He held an audience of over one thousand young athletes and their chaperones spellbound for approximately two hours. It was during that time that I sat in his audience that I made a commitment to myself to get into the professional speaking business. I had no idea how, because at that time I was a twenty-two-year-old produce clerk in a grocery store in Superior, Wisconsin.

"Another speaker who inspired me was J. Douglas Edwards. Edwards' memorable statement, 'Shut up! (and let the customer buy)' in one of his sales-training tapes, made all the difference in my life. He inspired me to go into and stay in the sales speaking profession."

Joe is a marvelous strategist. His favorite quotation, which he uses often in his programs is this:

> *"The heights that great men reached and kept*
> *Were not obtained by sudden flight,*
> *But they, while their companions slept,*
> *Were toiling upward in the night."*
>
> —*From Longfellow's*
> *"The Ladder of St. Augustine."*

Joe Charbonneau and his ability to see the right thing to do in any set of circumstances reminds me of a quotation by the famous attorney Louis Neizer: "In the still of the night, I slip into the camp of the enemy—and into their minds."

John W. Lee

As I deliberate about which speakers to share with you in this book who have most inspired me, I find difficulty in choosing. They are all so talented and smart I am dazzled! One of the brightest is John Wayne Lee. I enjoy John's humor and humble attitude mixed with his brilliant intelligence. He begins his program by asking for a show of hands to answer his opening time-management question: "How many of you are disorganized?"

John W. Lee
Organizational time management expert,
author/speaker/corporate consultant

Then John grins and says, "Now I want to see the hands of those of you who are *happily* disorganized!" Every hand goes up with a knowing laugh. Certainly including my own.

I especially admire John because when he married later in life and had his first child (a gorgeous baby boy) he insisted on taking him with him on every trip. What woman can resist a man who adores his children?

John was one of the first professional speakers to specialize in time/self-management. Millions have seen his TV specials, "Don't Agonize, Organize" and the "Challenge of Self-Management," on public broadcasting stations nationally. He has spoken worldwide for over four hundred of the Fortune 500 companies.

John told me he was inspired by Dr. Keith Davis, Professor Emeritus of Management, Arizona State University. Dr. Davis' books on human behavior and business continue to keep students and executives thinking about the importance of people and ways to utilize their talents and abilities. Dr. Davis was consulting editor of the McGraw-Hill Management Series and has been recognized with many honors.

John Lee said, "Dr. Davis was rated tops consistently by just about every group he has worked with because he practices what he teaches. His respect for each individual and their differences has always been clear, as was his thorough and thoughtful preparation. He talked about cultural diversity twenty years before it became an ethical and moral issue.

"Dr. Davis' speaking style was scholarly and low key. If you had read his books you probably found yourself intimidated—until he spoke. He held a conversation with his classes and his audiences. He asked more questions than all my doctoral professors combined. His classes always ended too soon.

"I thought of Dr. Davis when a disaster occurred as I was finishing my doctoral coursework and working at the Pepsi-Cola Management Institute," John continued.

"It was on the second day of our first top-management program, when it became clear our afternoon speaker could not get there in time to speak. The participants

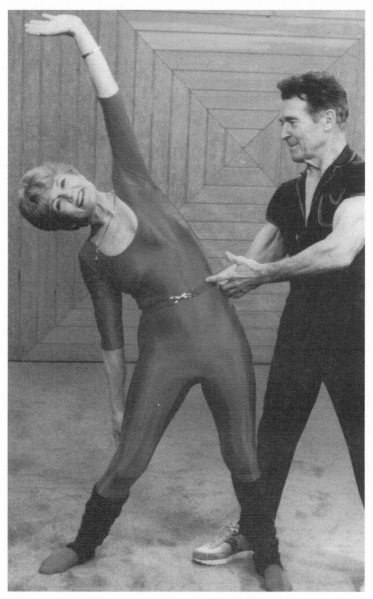

Jack and Elaine La Lanne
World-famous health, diet,
fitness authors/speakers

included Pepsi's senior executives from the president on down, as well as key bottlers. I was selected to present!

"Being twenty-six, much younger than my audience and talking to a group of hard-driving, critical, impatient, and very successful executives who had a tendency to walk out of the room if the speaker wasn't interesting, was highly stressful to say the least. Dr. Davis had gotten me my position at Pepsi. The entire university would know of my failure if I bombed.

"Retreating to my office and closing the door, I thought of writing my obituary, but ended up thinking of Dr. Davis' remarks after a session, which had been mainly interchange among the students. He said, 'The less I lecture the better the session. Do your research, ask good questions, make your audience think and learn.'

"I frantically put together a list of questions. Then I used a very low-key opening. I explained why I was taking the original speaker's place, that I was excited to have the opportunity to share some of the insights I had developed from my research on time management, but most of all I was pleased to learn from them.

Then I raised my questions and let them raise theirs. The ninety minutes flew by. Dr. Davis' lessons on involvement and participation have been part of every presentation I have given since. The more involvement and participation on the part of the audience and good questions raised, the more thinking and the higher the ratings and satisfaction."

Jack and Elaine La Lanne

This exciting speaking couple are two of the finest and most passionately enthusiastic speakers I have ever heard. As Merv Griffin says, they are "legends in their own time." No wonder CBS calls them the "fitness king and queen."

You may have seen Jack perform some of his miraculous physical feats on television. At age forty he swam the length of the San Francisco Golden Gate Bridge—underwater—with 140 pounds of equipment. A world record!

Patricia Ball
Board of Directors, NSA. Multi-talented actress,
communications specialist speaker, author

At sixty he swam from Alcatraz Island to Fisherman's Wharf, handcuffed, shackled, and towing a twenty-thousand-pound boat. At seventy Jack was handcuffed, shackled, then fighting strong winds and currents as he towed seventy boats with seventy people from the Queen's Way Bridge in Long Beach Harbor, California, to the Queen Mary, almost two miles.

Like so many great speakers, Jack and Elaine are enthusiastic crusaders about their subject, every moment of their lives. They convert doubters into believers of daily exercise and good nutrition with evangelical fervor.

My favorite La Lanne story is about how Jack began. He was a sickly high school teenager who happened to hear a health expert speaker named Paul Bragg. Jack was transformed. He determined to follow Bragg's advice exactly, and thus a great speaker, author, businessman, and health expert was born.

Jack is a fitness pioneer. He invented health equipment, opened chains of gyms, and has spoken all over the world. His lovely wife, Elaine, works with him side by side. I can't think of anyone in the speaking world who is more genuine, sincere, and dedicated to helping people become more than they ever dreamed of. As Lowell Thomas, himself a great speaker, said, "Jack La Lanne is one of the most versatile and entertaining speakers I have ever heard."

Sports Illustrated Magazine describes the La Lannes as "high on life!" So do I.

Patricia Ball

The first time I heard Patricia Ball speak, I realized that I was in the presence of a great actress as well as a fine speaker. She has portrayed many famous American women, such as Abagail Adams, with verve and excitement. Patricia is internationally well known for her in-depth seminars on many phases and aspects of communication. It is her experience in acting, television, radio, and stage, which brings such magic to her programs.

When I asked this lovely lady which speaker inspired her, she told me, "Dottie, I learned from many, studying

Michael Aun
Exciting sales speaker, winner, Toastmasters'
"World Champion Public Speaker" Award

their various styles. When I was very young I became fascinated with Eleanor Roosevelt. In my twenty-two years on the professional platform, I have worked to emulate her sense of humanity and personal warmth.

"Eleanor was often ridiculed. Her voice cracked and she used every note in the scale, often in one sentence. But the passion behind her delivery and her obvious honest desire to convince and move others set her up as my role model.

"I was surprised to learn that public speaking 'scared Eleanor to death.' She was a woman of great courage. If her speech could further a cause in which she believed, she forced herself to do what was hard for her.

"Born in an era when wives of political leaders were seen and not heard, she was far ahead of the times. She began to flower with the onset of Franklin Roosevelt's polio. I attribute my interest in gender difference and women's advancement to Eleanor, who revolutionized the role of 'First Lady.' She elevated the American woman to a new level of consciousness.

"My programs work for anyone who needs to be more persuasive and convincing. I speak to mainly male and mixed groups. However, I've had specific training in male/female communication styles. Some of my programs are aimed at helping women executives learn to break the 'glass ceiling.' Eleanor's message to women was 'get into the game and stay in it. Throwing mud from the outside won't help. Building up from the inside will.' I hope that I too will be remembered for my strong, ethical conscience and sense of humanity."

Michael A. Aun

Michael Aun is always introduced as a "world champion speaker" and rightfully so. He won this honor from Toastmasters International by defeating eight other speakers representing some 150,000 Toastmasters from the sixty-five-country Toastmaster International speaking world. He has shared the platform with three United States presidents and a host of celebrity speakers such as

Alan Cimberg
Famous U.S. sales expert, exciting motivator

Tom Peters, Paul Harvey, Dr. Norman Vincent Peale, and Art Linkletter.

Michael is a businessman who owns a construction business, a real estate development firm, a nationally acclaimed family-owned restaurant, and a very large insurance practice. His popular column, "Behind the Mike" has been syndicated for twenty years. Michael has a robust, down to earth style that especially appeals to me as a businesswoman.

When I asked him for his favorite quote by a speaker he gave me these two. From President Teddy Roosevelt, "Far better it is to have dared mighty things, to win glorious triumphs—even though checkered by failure—than to take rank with those poor spirits who neither enjoy much nor suffer much. For they live in a grey twilight that knows not victory nor defeat." And this one, from the gridiron at West Point, New York, "Upon these friendly fields of strife are sown the seeds that on other fields and on other days are borne the fruits of victory."

Michael is a wonderful entrepreneur. He offers convention meeting planners an unusual service, besides his excellent speaking. He brings his special camera and takes color still pictures of the attendees. Then during the banquet the pictures are shown on a big screen at one end of the hall. Of course everyone loves to see themselves.

Michael Aun explained that the speaker who has inspired him most is W Mitchell (featured in this book). Michael says, "What an inspiration W Mitchell is to everyone who knows him. He is a truly remarkable man who has dealt with adversity like no other human being I have ever met." Amen, Michael Aun, amen.

Alan Cimberg

Alan is one of the all-time great sales speakers. He is so full of vitality that everyone in the audience picks up his power surge instantly. He has shared the platform with Red Motley of *Parade Magazine*, with Dale Carnegie, Reverend Schuller, Earl Nightingale, and Paul Harvey of "The Rest of the Story" fame.

Alan told me he began speaking when he was suddenly called up to substitute for a another speaker. Like so many beginnings, he got his chance when the star was incapacitated. He received ten dollars for that first speech.

I love the way Alan has his audience singing "rounds" and standing up and sitting down to get them warmed up for his great message. A dynamo. He says he delivers basic truths, but always with tremendous energy. Alan's background as a sales manager for two AAA-1 rated companies gives him a wonderful platform of knowledge.

His favorite quote is, "Whatever you think you can do, begin it: boldness has genius, magic, and power in it." —Goethe.

The speaker who inspired the energetic Alan Cimberg is Dave Yoho. Alan told me: "The reasons why Dave Yoho inspired me are because he is a strong proponent of what I believe is the first path for speaking success— putting out energy. He espouses three other important qualities: One, self-discipline; two, optimism; and three, persuasiveness.

"Dave Yoho is a showman with a lot of pizzazz. Just visualize the average national political convention and the importance of pizzazz to it."

Alan continued, "I was also inspired by Dale Carnegie. I was part of a group he trained to be public speaking instructors a great many years ago.

"One of my own favorite quotes by Dale Carnegie is: 'Don't be afraid to give your best to what seemingly are small jobs. Every time you conquer one, it makes you that much stronger. If you do the little jobs well, the big ones tend to take care of themselves.'"

"Ben Franklin" aka Ralph Archbold

Ben comes back to life with
all his wisdom and charm

Chapter 15

Our speakers bureau has an unusual specialty. We book more than eighty-five speakers who work in costume as characters from history and fiction. They create a special ambiance and spirit to meetings as they bring the great characters of the past back to life. We call them our "Dead Speakers Society."

While I adore all of the speakers on the myriad subjects they present, I must confess these "characters" have a special place in my heart. Maybe because I have always been such an avid reader and delight in my friends of the mind whom I can now book to appear in person to delight audiences. Here are just a few of our brilliantly alive "dead speakers."

Ben Franklin aka Ralph Archbold

In chapter one I told you about how I first met Benjamin Franklin at the rural Baldwin Park Public Library, as I read Frank Bettger's book on sales. I can't thank Mr. Bettger enough for the introduction. I have a very large collection of Benjamin Franklin's works and books about Ben, as well as many busts and pictures here in my office. Just behind my desk is a large picture of Ben with that darling grin at the corner of his mouth and his kind, wise eyes looking at me as I work every day. When I get stuck with a problem, I mentally ask him what he would do. Ben Franklin is my special friend of the mind.

It is no wonder that Ben Franklin of Philadelphia, who wears the costume at all times, has his long hair cut in the Franklin style, and even has small square glasses with his own prescription in them, would immediately catch my attention. Ralph Archbold never steps out of character. He *is* Ben Franklin. He portrays Ben with fun and wisdom and is in great demand literally worldwide as a speaker.

Once I thought to play a joke on Ralph. I told him I was sure I had been Ben's lady friend, Madame Helvitus of France, in a past life.

"You remember me, Ben!" I said. "I held salons at my estate where I invited the most influential people of France to come and meet you.

"I helped you raise money for LaFayette's troops. Together we arranged to purchase the first U.S. naval vessel. We named it after your *Poor Richard's Almanac*— 'The Bon Homme Richard,' and we hired John Paul Jones to Captain it!

"Do you recall playing chess with me while we planned our strategy? I sat in my 'slipper' bathtub with a small heater under the instep, and we played chess on the table which more or less covered my chest! I was your love—your soulmate!"

Ben Franklin, aka Ralph Archbold, turned to me, winked, and said in a very mischievous way, "*Which* French lady did you say you were?"

Ralph Archbold has had recreated a musical instrument which Ben Franklin invented, the armonica. It consists of whirling glasses spun by use of a foot pedal, and played with wet fingers. Heavenly sweet music. Ralph plays it in some of his Franklin presentations. Franklin had an excellent voice and wrote many songs.

When the United States celebrated the anniversary of our Constitution, Ralph was chosen to appear in all of the advertisements of the Philadelphia Tourist and Convention Bureau. They sent him on a world publicity tour to talk about our much-beloved Constitution which has been used as a model for democracy by many countries.

Ralph told me his favorite Franklin quote is: "Be generous with that which costs little—sincere interest, friendship, and good counsel."

Of course the person who has inspired Ralph most is Franklin himself, but he was also inspired when he first heard Dr. Norman Vincent Peale speak. Ralph remembers: "Dr. Peale talked about the importance of sharing. He said that when you find something of value, the greatest pleasure you will ever have will be in sharing it with someone else.

"That thought changed everything for me. Till that point I had carefully guarded everything I valued, fearing that I would lose it if I shared it. After Dr. Peale's speech, I started practicing giving freely to others.

"I found that Dr. Peale was absolutely right. The greatest joy in life is definitely in the things we share. This thought led me to a career in speaking where I fulfill my obligation to give pleasure to others by sharing the things of value I have discovered."

Ben Franklin said: "The greatest joy in life is sharing ideas." (The name of the speakers magazine I publish is "Sharing Ideas." We blew a kiss to Ben Franklin when we chose the name.)

Ralph Archbold's latest success is a Philadelphia speakers bureau called the Colonial Collection. Besides booking Ben Franklin, Ralph arranges for performances at meetings and conventions by Paul Revere, Tom Jefferson, Betsy Ross, William Penn, and other famous people of that era.

My own adventurous study of everything about Benjamin Franklin has personally taught me many things. One is to find true delight in the success of all those around me. What is sadder than someone who is bitter because of someone else's success?

Another is not to worry because everyone on earth is not delighted by my success. This Franklin quote means a great deal to me. "Thank you, Lord, for the success of my friends—and the fewness of my enemies."

Mark Twain aka Roger Durrett

"An Evening with Mark Twain" is a treat for any audience. Roger Durrett brings Mark Twain back to life—on the Delta Queen and Mississippi Queen ships as they churn their way up the Mississippi—for universities, theaters, banquet halls, and for all kinds of meetings. Roger's serious interest in Twain encompasses a personal library which includes over 250 volumes on or about Twain; original photographs, autographs, and fifteen first editions.

Roger Durrett told me: "Dottie, as you know, any speaker who has 'trod the boards' has the good fortune

"Mark Twain" aka Roger Durrett
Witty Mark Twain lives anew

to meet with interesting people. Part of the fascination of portraying Mark Twain for me is the opportunity to make history real.

"It is part of the charm that comes from the audiences' willing suspension of disbelief that is so critical to what I attempt to do on stage.

"When I walk the streets of Hannibal, stand in the pilot house of a steamboat, or run my hand along the mantel at Mark Twain's home in Hartford, then for me history is made real. These are the special moments.

"One of the Twain lines that got me going was one I heard from Hal Holbrook as I saw him portray Twain when I was sixteen years old. Hal has been an inspiration to me in my Mark Twain journey. 'Ah, the dreams of our youth, how beautiful they are, and how perishable.'

"As an adult and as a speaker, I have met, talked to, corresponded with, and come to call Hal Holbrook 'friend.' A bit of the enchantment of our profession, don't you think? A piece of my own history made even more real by unforeseen subsequent events.

"My favorite quote is from Mark Twain. This is not a line that got me going, but one I discovered years into my research. It's simple, yet somehow the sentiment in it conveys an essence of the man for me. Wise, but not preachy, heartfelt, but not gushy: 'Wrinkles should only come to show where the smiles have been.'

"Was this a well-disguised paraphrase of the 'carpe diem' teachers pound into their students? Perhaps. Even at that tender age, I recognized the truth it contains.

"As to other quotations which have inspired me—like others my age, I can still hear the clear ring of the words, 'Let the word go forth from this time and place, that the torch has been passed to a new generation of Americans.'

"This line, for sheer eloquence, had an enormous impact on me as I discovered the power of the spoken word. It was from JFK's inaugural address. Some might argue that 'Ask not...' etc., was by far the more powerful of the words spoken that cold January day. But these 'Let the word go forth...' ones are those I remember personally as capturing the spirit of the moment."

"General Patton" aka Richard Pierce
The General leads business troops to victory

Roger Durrett told me he is also deeply inspired by Winston Churchill's magnificent "finest hour" speech.

Roger said, "I had occasion to work with and introduce former Prime Minister Edward Heath of England. Imagine my delight, (exhilaration is more the word) to sit one-on-one with a man who knew Winston Churchill personally as few ever would."

Roger recalled for me the occasion of Churchill's most famous speech: "Civilization hung in the balance that day. France had fallen. June of 1940 was as bleak a time in English history as one could imagine. Yet Churchill delivered a radio speech that galvanized a nation and rallied all the best qualities of the English will into a determination to fight on alone. I read that speech many times before finally hearing it on a recording."

General George Patton aka Richard Pierce

Dick Pierce has created a magnificent Gen. George S. Patton. Not only is his costume authentic to the last ribbon, medal, boots, crop, and gloves, his demeanor is rough, tough, and electrifying. One of the most appropriate places we have had the pleasure of booking "General Patton" was for an American meeting held at the General George Patton Hotel in Germany.

I have seen Dick Pierce, costumed perfectly as the general, stride on stage and say, "I understand this company is not winning the competitive *nor* the quality battle! I want this group to come to attention! I am going to lead this company to victory!"

His spirit fills the entire auditorium. What a man! Dick told me his favorite quote by General George Patton is, "Never take consul of your fears."

Dick told us that when he started in the speaking business some fifteen years ago, he was petrified that he would let the audience down. He said, "Had I not heeded ol' George's advice, my first speech might have been my last, because I'd never have walked out on that stage the first time. The odd thing is, I'm still scared every time, waiting there in the wings. I just control it better. Once

Chuck Kovacic as Sherlock Holmes

I'm on stage, the fear is gone in an instant. I guess that means I still care about putting on a good show.

"One of my favorite quotes by General Patton is, 'Wars may be fought with weapons, but they are won by people. It is the spirit of those who follow and of the one who leads that gains the victory.'"

Dick Pierce was inspired by hearing G. Gordon Liddy speak. Dick told us, "Gordon and I were on a program together in Orange County, California. He held the audience in the palm of his hand for three hours. I had to go on next and believe me, he was a tough act to follow. Fortunately, my kind of humor played well off of Liddy's program and all turned out well for both of us. It turned out that we both had a mutual friend—J. Edgar Hoover."

Sherlock Holmes aka Chuck Kovacic

If you have ever participated in a "mystery evening" you know what fun one can be. Chuck Kovacic as Sherlock Holmes quickly has an entire convention group looking for clues and using their minds to solve puzzles.

When you meet Sherlock personally, he shakes your hand and explains, "The reports of my death are unfounded! You see, actually there are no records of my death!" (He is a character of fiction; however, many people believe he truly lived.)

Every part of Chuck's Sherlock Holmes costume is authentic, even to the year of the English coin on his watch fob. Chuck is wonderful because he never steps out of character. You instantly slip into the past and begin the exciting game of "let's pretend."

Chuck knows so much about Sherlock and the several other "dead speakers" he portrays, that he can hold conversations and answer questions in an entertaining way for hours. He can step from one character to another in the twinkling of an eye and improvise like Jonathan Winters, quickly. An amazing talent!

He custom-tailors comedy programs where he portrays Will Rogers, Groucho Marx, and many other famous people for a galaxy of Fortune 500 companies worldwide. Chuck has been featured on many radio and TV shows

"Albert Einstein" aka Arden Bercovitz

Dazzles and charms audience
with "Einstein Live"

such as "CBS Morning News," "Night Court," "Superior Court," PBS, and "Entertainment Tonight."

When I asked Chuck to tell me about the speaker who inspired him most, he answered: "I've been inspired by instructors in school who enthralled their students with their grasp of topic and their ability to make it come alive. This spurred me to create an experience where a similar bond is created between the listener and the speaker as a storyteller. Hopefully I create a memory that will then continue to linger.

"This bond was a very large part of the success of Will Rogers. But the tradition of a great storyteller goes back much further. I sit enraptured listening to tapes of Joseph Campbell as he relates tales of long ago heros and their relationship to today. Both he and Will Rogers weave their audiences into webs of insight centered upon those traditions, one that I strive to continue."

Chuck's favorite quote is one of Will Rogers': "I never met a man I didn't like." Chuck explains, "I use a variation of this quote to help me interact with my guests when I say, 'I never met an audience that I didn't like.'

"These words sum up the interaction between audience and stage that I focus on in my presentations. 'A speaker in love with the audience is always a success.'"

Albert Einstein aka Arden Bercovitz

A man came up to talk to me after I spoke to an audience in San Diego about the world of paid speaking. He introduced himself as a scientist who worked at the famous San Diego Zoo's Center for the Reproduction of Endangered Species. Then he told me he had a dream. He wanted to bring his favorite character from history back to life—Albert Einstein.

Being an Einstein enthusiast myself, I was delighted. Arden Bercovitz has dark hair without the big bushy look of Einstein, but he told me he had all of the makeup worked out, and that there was such a wealth of Einstein material, he had much to choose from. Being a scientist himself, he felt close to Einstein's spirit.

214

"Roger the Barbarian" aka Dr. Roger Burgraff
Amazing program of strategy of ancient warriors

It was almost a year later that Arden attended my Speak & Grow Rich Seminar. I was so glad to see him bringing his dream to life. "Dr. Einstein" now speaks to corporate and association managers and executives, especially those in telecommunications, aerospace, engineering, computers, and education. High school and college science classes love him. He fields questions from the audience and answers them in the words of Einstein. His subject: "Thinking Bigger and Better, More Often."

Arden tells one of my favorite Einstein stories in such a visual way that everyone in the audience sees the details in the theater of their minds. As a young boy Albert Einstein dreamed of riding out into the deep blue of the universe seated on a ray of light and traveling at the speed of light. In one hand he held a clock, in the other a mirror. That dream was the birth of Einstein's theory of relativity.

Arden Bercovitz told me that besides Einstein, the speaker who inspired him most is Jim Rohn.

"Dottie, in Rohn's audience, I have always had the experience that he is talking directly to me, no matter who else was there. His presentation style is distinct and dramatic, and only outdone by an admirable flare with concepts. My favorite Jim Rohn quote is this one: 'Sometimes we try to make up in words what we lack in self-confidence. Part of the key to being brief is personal development, growth, awareness, and an understanding of self-worth. Now you can see the economy of words. This is a good position to be in, when what you are adds so much weight to what you say, you don't have to say very much.'"

I often use this Einstein favorite quote of mine when I talk to new speakers just beginning their careers: "Try not to become a person of success, but rather try to become a person of value."

"Roger the Barbarian" aka Roger Burgraff

If you sat here in my speakers bureau office in Glendora, California, and Roger Burgraff walked in, you would see a tall, handsome, educated man whose specialty at Loma Linda Hospital has been to teach those who have lost their vocal cords because of cancer to speak again. Not only is Dr. Burgraff a famous healer in the medical field, he has had extensive acting training, and is a student of history.

As you shake his hand, you might catch a twinkle in his eye. I know you would delight as I do in his funny and moving stories of the lessons we can learn from the leaders of yesterday. This refined, charming man is the famous "Roger the Barbarian!"

We have booked Roger literally all over the world with his humdinger program on "Learning to Lead Like a Barbarian."

He portrays the role of the Barbarian wearing a metal helmet complete with horns, and a costume and spear to match. Dr. Burgraff's study of the master archetypal behaviors of great, passionate, barbarian leaders, rulers, warriors, wizards, and lovers has produced amazing information.

At first blush, you may recoil and ask, "What could my group learn from the leader of a hoard of savages?" The answer is: "A whole lot."

Roger explains in his fascinating programs that Attila the Hun's success lay in his ability to delegate, while he concentrated on a larger goal—in his case the gigantic task of uniting the Huns.

Dr. Roger Burgraff's intense study of historic leaders has revealed this: "A true leader cannot lead alone. He empowers others to lead. One of the toughest jobs is to develop subordinates—not only to get the job done, but to cultivate competent chieftains to take over while another leader moves up to higher responsibility."

When I asked Dr. Burgraff to explain to me how he sees modern business, he said to me: "Dottie, business, like war, can be hell, especially in today's aggressive marketplace. More than ever you must have a keen sense of competition to stay on top. Learn to negotiate, size up your enemies, and learn from your mistakes. Don't let defeat stop you."

Points Roger makes about the timeless leadership principles of the brilliant Queen Boadicea of Brittain, Genghis Khan, Attila, and other barbarians are: "Mastering the skills to lead in turbulent times, targeting your vision, accomplishing your mission, and empowering your people to take initiative and accept responsibility.

One of my own favorite historical leaders is Queen Boadicea. Ceasar's legions made her watch while they raped and killed off her entire family. They thought she would be forever broken in spirit. But Boadicea rose up, put on her armor, and led her armies herself into battle. My kind of woman.

Dr. Roger Burgraff said he was inspired by the lovely speaker, Glenna Salsbury of Arizona. Roger took to heart Glenna's advice, "Cream rises to the top not because of what it does, but because of what it is."

Roger presents many programs for dynamic Jimmy Calano, CEO of CareerTrack Seminar company. Roger is greatly inspired by this advice from Mr. Calano. "It's not what you know, it's what you do with what you know."

How true. We all know people who live out their lives in the "starving artist mode" because they refuse to understand how to combine talent with business skills. Frankly, I have never met a person of accomplishment who was not criticized, ridiculed, or put down because of their ideas. Roger has this sign over his desk at his office:

"Great Spirits have always encountered violent opposition from mediocre minds."
—Albert Einstein

Faith Popcorn
"Nostradamas of Marketing" author, "The Popcorn Report" predicts marketing trends

Chapter 16

Faith Popcorn

Faith is known as the "Nostradamus of marketing." She is a brilliant practitioner of observation, deduction, and prediction. American business says: "Faith Popcorn said this would happen years ago!"

She believes that most businesses, no matter what they sell, will soon also package information. Her coined word "cocooning" is now listed in four dictionaries. It means working, creating, purchasing—all done without leaving our homes. Faith tracks trends and predicts business futures.

When I had the privilege of interviewing Faith Popcorn for our speakers publication, *Sharing Ideas Newsmagazine*, I was stunned by her visions into the future of business. No wonder her "brain reserve trends" are the subject of much media coverage. She is frequently interviewed by *Time, Fortune*, the "Today Show," "Face the Nation," "CNN," and many more important publications and media productions.

Her speaking style is low key, her ideas brilliant. I began my interview with her with the same question she must be asked by most interviewers: "Is Faith Popcorn your real name, and if not, how did you give yourself this unique title?"

Faith told me, "Dottie, my favorite last name story is about when my great-great-grandfather came over from Italy (he was a neighbor to Lee Iacocca's great-great-grandfather). When he went through Ellis Island immigration, they asked him his name. 'My name is Poppa Corne,' he told them with his heavy accent."

Faith has several funny stories about her name. Another is that her first real boss, Gino Garlanda, had trouble and fun trying to pronounce her family name, which is Plotkin. He lovingly dubbed her "Popcorn."

I asked Faith about the future of meetings and what the convention of tomorrow will be like. She replied: "The convention of tomorrow will still be an important function. People who often work in a solitary manner at home need face-to-face contact. Especially so as more and more people 'cash out' and 'cocoon.' Some speakers may present a special program as a hologram. This presentation can be put on a video tape and run through a machine. Remember 'Star Wars'?"

Since ninety-five percent of all the speakers in the world operate their businesses from home offices, "cocooning" is of great interest. I asked Faith what she saw ahead for this modern business trend. She said, "We predicted 'cocooning' in the early '80s. Through our customer interviews, reading, watching, and listening, we saw growing dissatisfaction. People were burning out and longed to be at home. They were not doing it yet, but we told our clients to start making things available for the home and the home office and business.

"We predicted the huge markets for take-out food, home delivery of groceries, home entertainment, and shipping. We see a two-billion-dollar take-out-food business emerging. Over seventy-five percent of homes have VCRs. Soon we'll have access to five hundred cable channels. Fifty-five million homes have QVC shopping network. One hundred million people shop through catalogs."

Faith continued, "The brain reserve trend, which means cashing out everything you own in a big city, moving to a small country town, and doing business via modem, fax, and delivery service, is a big one for speakers and the speakers bureau industry who often form home offices. We tracked this trend as we watched the life pace become faster and faster. People reset priorities from just work to personal and family health and happiness, with more free time to enjoy life and get rid of stress.

"With today's technological advances, it is easy and pleasant to work from home. People now put more trust in themselves and enjoy new-found freedom by being their own boss."

Faith Popcorn is one of the most fascinating speakers on the platform today. She is not only a great speaker, she creates her own crystal ball, which allows business to see what she sees is coming. Her book, *The Popcorn Report,* published by Harper Business, has changed the way America does business.

My favorite Popcorn quote is: "The future waits for no man, no woman, no company."

Stew Leonard, Jr.

Here is a young man who practices all the ideas Faith Popcorn visualizes. Stew Leonard's Dairy store, in Norwalk, Connecticut, has reaped worldwide recognition for customer service. Audiences from many countries seek Stew as a speaker because they want to learn about his unique ideas—his tools for making customers very happy. Well over one hundred thousand customers a week frequent the aisles of his store, producing one hundred million dollars in annual sales.

The policy of his store is: "Rule number one: The customer is always right. Rule number two: If the customer is ever wrong, reread rule number one."

We asked Stew Leonard how he began speaking. He told us his first invitation to speak came from Sam Malone of Milliken Textiles. Sam invited Stew to come and speak to his management group. On the night before the program, Stew asked to see the room where he would speak the next day. To his great surprise, he was ushered into a meeting room set up for an audience of four hundred.

On either side of him on the program were Buck Rodgers, the retired senior vice president of IBM, and Joe Girard, listed by the *Guinness Book of World Records* as the world's number one car salesman.

Stew Leonard told us: "The man who was doing the high-tech side of the show said to me, 'Where are your slides?'

"He took one out, looked at it, and said, 'Who took these?' I replied, 'Why I took them all myself, right around the store.'

"He shook his head and said, 'These are the most unprofessional slides I've ever had to work with.' My heart sank.

"You see, my slides were not glass-mounted. I didn't know what a glass-mount was."

Stew Leonard, Jr.
Top U.S. expert, customer service

Next morning Stew went on anyway. "As I stepped off of the stage a production manager smiled and shook my hand. He said 'Stew, don't change a thing. Your slides match your speech.'

"The next morning at the store a speakers bureau called to ask me if I could manage six programs a year.

"My first date for the bureau was with Domino's Pizza. Afterwards I sat and talked to the client about our businesses. We each walked away with pages of notes!

"Once a former United States presidential speech-writer was in my audience. I had met him before, so I asked if he would critique my talk. He gave me pages and pages of notes. 'Don't put your hand in your pocket. Don't scratch your head. Don't say 'um.'

"It was Paul Newman who finally set me straight. My store sells his salad dressing. He told me, 'Stew, don't listen to them. Speak from the heart. Speak about something you love talking about. Get into it what you are doing with your great store.'

"Now I do fifty or more professional programs a year, all from the heart."

Jeff Slutsky

Jeff Slutsky is world famous for his marketing program titled, "Confessions of a Streetfighter." When I first heard that title, I thought he might be a wise-guy. Well, Jeff is wise alright, but not in that sense. He is conscientious, hard working, customer-oriented, and knows his stuff.

His background is in advertising and public relations, with personal entrepreneurial experience. He discovered and developed result-oriented, low-cost tactics to build sales. His shrewd thinking, innovative problem solving, and brilliant ideas on how to do business on a shoe-string make him a very popular speaker with our speakers bureau clients.

Jeff has been featured in the *Wall Street Journal, INC Magazine* and *USA Today*. One of my favorite streetfighting stories is the one Jeff tells about the high couture beauty salon owner whose shop was in a mall.

Jeff Slutsky
Author/speaker "Streetfighter"
International sales expert

A "low-price" competitor opened up right across from him. Their first move was to put up a big banner which read, "Great permanent waves. CHEAP!"

The fancy salon owner was in agony, until he got an idea. He went out and ordered an even bigger banner than the new shop displayed. When it arrived he hung it across his front window. It read: "We FIX cheap permanents!"

I asked Jeff Slutsky to tell us his favorite quote. He said, "Dottie, it is from the late Howard Shenson, the great consulting and speaking guru. He helped me get started over fifteen years ago when I was consulting and conducting seminars. Those business activities led me into speaking.

"Howard Shenson told me, 'We are in the information business. Clients buy this information in a variety of media or formats. All of these have a synergistic effect on your career. Speeches, seminars, newsletters, consulting, audio and video tapes, and books should all be part of your speaker product mix.'"

Jeff told us that Michael Le Boeuf, Ph.D., is the greatest speaker he has ever heard for a number of reasons. Jeff says, "When I think of a speaker I think of the speaker's message. It can be delivered in a speech, tapes, books, videos, and so on. Dr. Le Boeuf is a genius at integrating all of these avenues to provide great impact for his audiences. His message, which inspired me tremendously, is: 'Actions that get rewarded, get done.'

"I have learned that everything else in business evolves around that one great thought."

We enjoy working with Jeff, a true professional in every way.

Tom Winninger

Tom is a fine business speaker who specializes in America's food industry. He speaks on the subjects of strategic management, customer service, sales, and marketing techniques. I love his motto: "Why compete when you can win!"

Tom Winninger
Past President, NSA, dynamic business speaker

Tom is a prolific writer who has been published in over fifty trade journals. He has served as president of the National Speakers Association.

Tom told me that he was very inspired by Bishop Sheen's television show, "Life is Worth Living." Bishop Sheen's show was immensely popular and soon had skyrocketing ratings. It was the only television show that ever knocked the popular "The Milton Berle Show" off the air. Bishop Sheen had the rare ability to take complex philosophical and theological concepts and translate them into language and lessons all audiences of every faith could understand.

Tom's favorite quotes are these by Bishop Sheen: "Credibility and behavior are twins. Only the one who practices convictions is believable." "It's what you give away that makes you wealthy, not what you keep."

Nido Qubein

The first time I heard Nido Qubein speak was at a speaker's showcase in Atlanta. Nido was newly graduated from college and had a youthful charm about him that everyone loved. He told the story of his arriving in the United States at age seventeen to go to college. He spoke very little English.

Nido decided that the people in the local churches might like to hear what the Holy Land is really like from a boy who was born and raised there. He booked himself to speak at the churches and was taken to the hearts of the people. They not only paid him, they took up collections for him.

They asked him to speak to their youth groups. He became a church youth director and gave his programs on local radio. Before long his radio shows were syndicated across the country. Nido saw that there was a need for materials for Christian youth leaders, so he started a small publishing company and sold his publications via direct mail to churches across the country. Soon Nido was able to bring his love from Lebanon. They were married and are raising a beautiful family.

Nido Qubein
Past President, NSA, Lebanese-American who
made U.S. dream of opportunity come true

The speaker who first inspired Nido is Ty Boyd. Nido was twenty-four years old when he heard Ty speak at a Civitan International convention in Boston. Ty had that twinkle in his eye and a smile that warmed the audience.

Nido told me, "Ty spoke with a gentle voice. He had a confident personality and a simple message that made his audience laugh. He inspired us. His delivery was flawless, his gestures immaculate. I thought, 'There is a professional.'

"I had just started my publishing business with the five hundred dollars I had saved while working my way through school. I asked if I could spend a few minutes with Ty. He agreed, and I asked him a million questions, which he answered brilliantly. We live an hour apart in North Carolina and are close friends."

Today Nido is an international speaker, businessman, and author of thirty books. As Dr. Norman Vincent Peale said, "Nido Qubein is proof that the American dream is still alive."

The quotations which inspired Nido most are these: "Nothing in the world can take the place of persistence. Talent will not; nothing is more common than unsuccessful people with talent. Education will not; the world is full of educated derelicts. Persistence and determination alone are omnipotent." —Calvin Coolidge.

"I cannot believe that the purpose of life is merely to be happy. I think the purpose of life is to be useful, to be responsible, to be honorable, to be compassionate. It is, above all, to matter: to count, to stand for something, to have it make some difference that you lived at all." —Leo Rosten.

Ty Boyd

I have enjoyed hearing my good friend Ty Boyd speak many times, but I think the time he made the biggest impression on me was when I passed the door of an auditorium in which I was speaking on the same day. I saw a thousand people in his audience all wearing T-shirts imprinted with the words "No More Alibis" on them.

Ty Boyd
Past President, NSA, TV personality,
fascinating business speaker

These words are the title of Ty's marvelous talk for sales organizations. All of us put off doing the great things we are capable of by giving alibis, not only to others, but to ourselves. Just the sight of those people and that phrase repeated one thousand times, gave me new resolve to dust off some dreams I had let slide to the back of life. Ty told me one of his favorite quotes is by John Wesley, "Make all you can, save all you can, and give all you can."

Ty has served as president of the National Speakers Association. He is not only talented, but he is a good friend to all who are fortunate to know him. I have never heard him utter a mean or hurtful word. He comes from the world of television and the electronic media. Many recognize his voice and cheerful smile.

The speaker who inspired Ty Boyd is Charlie Cullen. Ty said to me, "Dottie, Charlie Cullen was one of the most powerful, colorful, and effective professional speakers around during the fifties and sixties. He spoke to sales and management audiences around the world, from Carnegie Hall to Hong Kong.

"Most of Charlie's messages centered on the theme 'Getting a Bigger Bite Out of Life.' He thrilled, entertained, and inspired. His most famous story told of an inexperienced automobile salesperson who skillfully sold Charlie a big white Cadillac convertible—in the middle of winter—and made him love it!

"The Sales Congresses, which were so popular in the early sixties, featured Charlie Cullen, Dr. Ken McFarland, Bill Gove, Dr. Herb True, Fred Herman, (and as the first woman speaker for that group) Dottie Walters, among others. None inspired an audience more than Charlie.

"Charlie helped me to believe that I could be an effective presenter too. One evening, after a banquet at our local YMCA (Charlie had MC'd and I spoke) he asked me to wait and talk. We walked to our cars in the parking lot. He stopped, put his arm around my shoulder, and said 'Ty, you can do what I do.'

"How exciting! What he had done for me was what Babe Ruth might have done for a youngster hoping some day to play in the big leagues. 'You can hit in the bigs.'

"That night's experience said to me that I was no longer a young broadcaster who sometimes spoke, but a real honest-to-goodness speaker who also broadcasts. Wow! What a life-changing experience.

"Ever since that night, I've been trying to help others, whatever their field of choice, to discover that they can 'play in the big leagues' too. What a discovery!"

Ty told me another of his favorite quotes—one which many of us in this business love: "Whatever the mind can conceive and believe, it can achieve." —Napoleon Hill.

Incidentally, I discovered who inspired Napoleon Hill. It was Marcus Aurelieus of ancient Rome who said, "Whatever the mind can conceive, it can achieve." Napoleon Hill added the important phrase, "and believe."

Gene Perret
Top humorist/author, writer for Bob Hope and
many celebrity humorists

Chapter 17

Gene Perret

Gene Perret is one of the country's premier comedy writers and speakers. He has won three Emmys and is Bob Hope's head writer for all of Bob's television specials and personal appearances. Gene began writing comedy for Phyllis Diller, Mickey Shaughnessy, Slappy White, and others. He was a writer for "Laugh-In," "The Bill Cosby Show," "The Carol Burnett Show," "Welcome Back Kotter," "Three's Company" and "The Tim Conway Show."

Gene traveled with Bob Hope at the invitation of Queen Elizabeth II to write the Command Performance Show at the London Palladium on the occasion of the twenty-fifth anniversary of the Queen's Coronation. He has traveled with Bob Hope and his USO troupe to Beirut, Lebanon, the Persian Gulf, Saudi Arabia, Berlin, and Moscow.

Gene has a wit and warmth that delights audiences as he tells of his personal experiences with the great comedians. He is the author of thirteen books on comedy and is well known for his articles on humor in the *Reader's Digest* and many other publications.

Gene believes that humor is the message. He says, "Humor is an essential. We absolutely require it in today's hectic world. It is the safety valve that keeps us from taking the whole damn thing too seriously. We need mirth makers. We need humorous speakers who can get an audience to laugh with them and at them. When I traveled with Bob Hope, believe me, no one in the battle zones asked us, 'Why are you telling jokes?'"

When I asked Gene which speakers inspired him, he told me, "Dottie, as a youngster I read everything available about Will Rogers. I listened to Bob Hope, Red Skelton, Jack Benny, and other comics on the radio. I wanted to be a respected humorist like Will Rogers, or a successful comedian like Bob Hope, but I never tried.

Stan Freberg
Award-winning humorist/advertising genius,
author of *It Only Hurts When I Laugh*

"No one would applaud me, I thought. The professionals wouldn't welcome a beginner into their inner sanctum. Why even bother to try?

"I had the desire and the potential talent; what I didn't have was the courage. Then I heard Earl Nightingale speak. He said that anyone could think their way to success, that the power of the mind could accomplish miracles.

"His message changed my life. For the first time I not only had permission to try, but also encouragement. Earl Nightingale convinced me that I had as much right to follow my dreams as anyone else. I listened to his recordings time and time again. I followed my dreams and—Earl was right—a few of them came true.

"The quote that has affected me most in my writing and speaking career is from Napoleon Hill, but I first heard it quoted by Earl Nightingale: 'Whatever the mind of man can conceive and believe, it can achieve.'"

Stan Freberg

Remembering Stan from our high school days together at Alhambra, California, I think of him as the funniest kid I ever met. He was tall and skinny, with a blond "Afro" hairdo. He didn't have to act funny. He was naturally funny.

He wrote material for our school assemblies, did funny voices, was always involved in performing. Meanwhile, I was the feature editor and advertising manager for the *Alhambra High Moor*, our school newspaper.

The story of what happened to my schoolmate Stan Freberg after high school is amazing! Stan took the big red streetcar into Hollywood and found a job doing funny voices for Warner Brothers cartoons.

Then he wrote for and performed in the TV show "Time For Beany." Stan played "Cecil, the Sea Sick Sea Serpent." He and the other writers and performers had no office. They wrote the scripts the night before each show in coffee shops, parked cars, and in an office in a condemned building. The show won three Emmys.

Then Stan opened his Freberg Ltd. (but not very) advertising company. This kid from Alhambra High

School, with no formal marketing training, no degree from Harvard or any other business school, ran up a string of marketing successes that dumbfounded Madison Avenue.

He increased the sales of Coca Cola Bottling Company of Los Angeles by using a marketing strategy never tried before, increasing their business from a one-fifth share of the market to a half-share.

His campaign for the prune industry, "Today the pits, tomorrow the wrinkles" is an advertising classic that boosted prune sales by four hundred percent according to the *Wall Street Journal*. His unique campaign for the *Encyclopedia Britannica* resulted in sales of their books that helped them to declare that year as the most successful in their history.

Stan is a comedy writer whose book, *It Only Hurts When I Laugh*, (Times Books) is a best-seller. He is a famous, hysterically funny speaker. He writes music and award-winning advertising copy.

Stan told me the reason for his success is that he did have a lot of training—as a consumer. He creates ad campaigns to appeal to himself.

Stan told me, "Dottie, my work was greeted like a Frank Lloyd Wright building, thrust up overnight in a sea of Victorian architecture. The ad people did not understand me. But they understood sales results. *Advertising Age Magazine* selected my Contadina Tomato Paste campaign as one of the two top marketing success stories of the year."

Stan tells his audiences, "I ask myself if an ad, commercial, or marketing approach would appeal to me. I refuse to go with anything that wouldn't! Communication is the key—what it is really all about. Not for nothing did I name the course I taught at U.S.C. "Freberg on Communications."

Stan certainly is one of the most brilliant speakers and creative thinkers I have ever known. As Ray Bradbury wrote for Stan's great book, "Stan is like a very polite tailor asking the emperor how his skin feels now that his clothes are off."

Tom Ogden

Many speakers draw upon their background as leaders of industry and business, or as artists, athletes, or coaches for their speaking subjects. Other speakers step up onto the speaking platform from another part of the world of entertainment. Such a performer is master magician and comedian, Tom Ogden.

Tom is well known in the world of magic for his columns which appear in international magic magazines. He has received numerous awards from the world famous Magic Castle in Los Angeles for his work there. When we visited his magic performances at this exciting location, I was struck with watching him off stage. He constantly helped, made suggestions to, and encouraged the other performers. He is that kind of man.

Tom Ogden brings over twenty years of performance experience to the speaking platform with his "Magic of Creative Problem Solving" subject. He has appeared on dozens of talk shows in the United States, Australia, and Africa. He has been seen on "Days of Our Lives," "General Hospital," and "Superior Court," and has starred in several major commercials.

He is the author of several books on magic, and is the author of a tremendous new work, *200 Years of The American Circus, From Aba-Daba to the Zoppe-Zavatta Troupe,* published by Facts on File.

As a speakers bureau owner, I am always impressed with Tom's professional response: His press kits show up faster than normal, he always arrives at the venue hours before he needs to. He is the ultimate professional performer. When I asked Tom which speaker had influenced him, he said: "My entire entertainment career can be traced back to my first performing tour with a circus at the age of seventeen.

"Dr. Charles W. Boas is not a speaker in the usual sense. From 1969 through 1977, he owned and managed Circus Kirk, the all-student circus which toured the northeastern United States. He holds several college degrees. However in the 1950s he traveled with many major circuses. His dream was to own his own show. Circus Kirk was this dream come true.

Tom Ogden
Award-winning Magic Castle master magician/
creativity speaker, author circus encyclopedia

"I first saw Doc 'speak' on the 'bally platform'—a sheet of plywood on sawhorses in front of a sideshow tent. In the first half of his 'keynote' he gave a ten-minute 'bally,' as the 'pitch' is called in circus lingo.

"The bally's aim is to draw the 'towners' out of line for the Big Top and over into the sideshow. After the doors were opened to the tent, Doc switched to a 'grind'— a droning repetitive talk ('it's all on the inside; now is the time; this is the place; up one side and down the other; it's never out; it's never over; you go round and round like a merry-go-round') which eventually wore down the resistance of those few folks remaining on the circus midway.

"To perform an effective bally, the 'outside talker' must combine personal charisma with information, humorous entertainment, and a whole bunch of persuasion. No one does it better than Doc.

"Years later when I saw him give more traditional talks to circus fans and other associations, I understood why he was so effective. Not only did he have a complete understanding of and love for the circus, he had a passion to share his vision and experiences."

Tom Ogden also appears at conventions and for associations as that showman of all showmen, P.T. Barnum! Tom's whimsical, witty humor and top professionalism are not only magic, they are as welcome and lively as a magician's rabbit.

Gene Mitchener

For years Gene Mitchener dreamed of becoming a stand-up comic, but being in a wheelchair, his dream seemed impossible. As a disabled individual, he felt that he was drowning daily in a sea of negativity concerning what he could or could not do, where he could or could not go, or what he should or should not be able to achieve in his life. One day Gene decided not to allow what he couldn't do to stand in the way of what he could do.

He bills himself as "America's Only Sit-Down Comic!" Ever since he decided to live his dream no matter what, he and his wheelchair have been "on a roll," as *People*

Gene Mitchener
Funny, inspirational "sit-down"
wheelchair comic

Magazine reported. Gene is very much in demand, telling attendees at meetings and conferences, "When things get heavy... lighten up!"

Gene's ability to encourage and inspire his audiences to overcome obstacles in their lives has helped many to reach their goals and achieve their dreams. He turns personal pain into positive experience. He sees the funny side of every situation.

I think what captures my heart most about Gene is that while he is very funny, he has a riveting message. Gene says, "Do not let your physical or mental handicaps keep you from achieving your dreams."

Gene has been featured in hundreds of newspapers and magazines and is the recipient of the prestigious Variety Arts Award from the John F. Kennedy Center for the Performing Arts in Washington, D.C.

When I asked Gene which speaker inspired him most he said, "A lady from Phoenix, Arizona, Rita Davenport. She has an attitude that everything in life can be okay. I have tried to live my life by the same principal. Example: Concerning her husband looking at other women, Rita laughs and says, 'Those women don't have anything that I can't have fixed.'"

Recently when Gene spoke at a high school where the students were unruly, he turned his mike on full blast and said, "Listen here! Do I have to get up and come down there and straighten you kids out?" Stunned silence. Then they all laughed together and Gene went on with his delightful program.

This man makes everyone smile and laugh and realize that trouble is not a reason to quit. Yet he was so badly misformed at birth that his older brother, having expected and looking forward to a brother he could play ball with, asked his parents if they could please take Gene back and exchange him for a baby that was not broken.

Gene told me his favorite quote by a speaker is one he personally hangs on to: King Solomon in Proverbs 15:13, 14: "A merry heart doeth good like a medicine and a bittered and angered heart drieth and kinderith the bones."

Gene Mitchener, with his merry heart and his unbroken spirit, is a joy and a blessing to all who know him.

Cella Quinn
Speaker/author, who overcame tremendous
physical problems with true grit
to become financial genius

Cella Quinn

Cella Quinn perfectly personifies Aristotle's description of a great speaker as "a great person, who happens to speak well."

Whoever said, "What you do speaks so loudly we cannot hear what you say," understood the necessity for a speaker to be a person of character first, a speaker second. Who can not be moved by hearing her true story of guts, determination, hard work, and dreams?

She was raised on a farm. But unlike her sisters and brothers, she could not talk. She was born with a cleft palate which left her unable to speak. The roof of her mouth and the sides of her gums were filled with misplaced teeth, which caused her continuous pain. She walked with her head down, stayed at the back of the room, and carried a tablet and pencil with her always, in order to communicate.

But Cella had a dream. She grew vegetables and asked her younger brothers and sisters to sell them at their farm stand along the road. She saved her pennies until at last when she was sixteen, she took her life savings of forty-four dollars and headed for the bus station. She asked for the cheapest ticket to the largest city, determined to find a way to get her mouth and face fixed.

She found a room at the Y and a job at a Walgreen's drugstore lunch counter in Lincoln, Nebraska. She washed dishes with her back to the counter so that the customers would not see her face. She enrolled in secretarial school after work. Cella taught the other girls at the Y how to save money and formed an investment group.

Cella listened and watched everything around her. A dentist came in to Walgreens for breakfast every morning. She screwed her courage to the sticking place and wrote him a note. She told him how much her teeth ached.

"I can't pay you a lot," she wrote, "but I can pay you five dollars a month. Please help me."

The dentist took her to the University of Nebraska School of Dentistry where the students took her on as their special project. Their graduate department made her one of the first plastic palates in the world. It enabled her to begin to speak. They sent her to their speech therapy department. She saved every dollar, cleaned offices at night, and finally accumulated three thousand dollars for plastic surgery for her mouth and face.

Soon after the operation she got a better job. For the first time she could look people in the face. Then she immediately began college classes at night. Cella joined Toastmasters, whose members took her under their wings and lovingly helped her.

Today Cella Quinn is a famous speaker. She has became the vice-president of Smith Barney, Harris Upham and Company. She is a lifetime member of Smith Barney's Presidents Club, the first woman to ever make that rank. She now has her own investment company.

What Cella did, and does, speaks loudly. She is one of the most powerful speakers I have ever heard. She not only solved her own gigantic problems, she spends her life helping others to solve theirs. I am so proud of her.

This magnificent woman, who always has a smile and an encouraging word for everyone, told me that she loves this quote from Sophie Tucker: "From birth to age eighteen a girl needs good parents. From eighteen to thirty-five she needs good looks. From thirty-five to fifty-five she needs a good personality. From fifty-five on, she needs good cash! I've been rich and I've been poor; rich is better."

Cella told me, "The speaker who inspired me most spoke at my mother's funeral. This man told of how our lives are like a tapestry. As we pass through life, our travels are always under the loom. We see the black threads, with an occasional hint of gold and silver, grays and pinks. But it is after we die that we look down on the tapestry of the life that we have lived, and we see the full beauty of what we have woven."

Brian Tracy
Business genius, author, star Nightingale
Conant audio album international speaker

Chapter 18

Brian Tracy

The first word that comes to my mind about Brian Tracy is "Renaissance man." Here is a speaker who is so multi-talented that he is a role model in every way.

By the age of twenty-four he became vice-president of an international investment company. Then a successful automobile importer and distributor, establishing sixty-five dealerships. Real estate, sales, marketing, advertising, management, and consulting are all fields in which he is a champion.

Brian Tracy is a best-selling author/narrator for the giant audio/video publisher, Nightingale-Conant Corporation. His fourteen-volume "Effective Manager" seminar series is one of the best multi-media training programs in America. His "Psychology of Achievement" audio series is perhaps the most popular instructional audio program of all time, having sold more than 500,000 copies. He speaks to over 100,000 people in his seminars each year as he travels, works, and speaks in more than eighty countries.

No one makes a sound while Brian is speaking. He so fills each minute while he is on the platform with valuable content that the entire audience is hushed, alert, and concentrated.

Brian has set up independent distributors for his products. To give you an idea of his marketing genius, he told us that his producers sell in excess of five million dollars yearly, which doubles annually. He revealed that he spends twenty to thirty hours a week "staying on top of his materials."

When I asked Brian which speaker had inspired him, he said: "Zig Ziglar, Denis Waitley, Tom Peters, Ty Boyd, Don Hutson, Charles Plumb, Jim Cathcart, Tom Hopkins, John Boyle, Ken Blanchard, Dr. Norman Vincent Peale, and many others. The greatest impression they made on me in every case was the power of the spoken word to

Sol Rothstein
Rabbi, Chaplain Los Angeles Police Department,
expert "Handling Difficult People"

inform, motivate, entertain, and inspire me to do better and be better in some way.

"The result of hearing a good professional speaker is that people learn how to change and improve their lives, their work, and their relationships. Great speakers raise one's aspirations, hopes, and ambitions."

It is my personal experience with Brian Tracy that he is a gentleman and a good friend.

Here is Brian's favorite quote: "The greatest revolution of my generation is the discovery that by changing the inner attitudes of your mind, you can change the outer aspects of your life." —William James

Sol Rothstein

Sol is one of the most learned and wise men I have ever met. He is a rabbi, writer, eloquent speaker, and a loving friend to all he meets.

Sol tells the story of how he became a rabbi. Like many speakers he was inspired by a great person in his life. Just before the Korean War, Sol was assigned to the tank corps. As the ship was to sail, the chaplain at the base learned that his assistant was being discharged. Sol had attended services on a regular basis, so the chaplain asked for Sol as the replacement. Kismet! Sol was taken off the boat headed for Korea.

Eighteen-year-old Sol was inspired not only by the rhetoric, but also by the compassionate way Rabbi Wolf Gunther Plaut counseled people who came for help. Some soldiers were afraid or unhappy, others disillusioned, or disappointed. The rabbi gave them all hope by making each person believe in himself. He said, "It is not enough to say we believe in God. We must first believe in the talent God gave each of us."

Sol watched as the rabbi disarmed angry people with a sense of humor, and the young man thought, "Oh, if only I could be that way."

He worked as the rabbi's assistant for four months. Then the rabbi was suddenly granted an emergency furlough because of a serious home problem. Sol was

Gary Yamamoto
Japanese-American business expert,
author, speaker

shocked to learn he had been assigned to take the rabbi's place as chaplain.

He protested, "I'm not a rabbi, only a kid! What do I know about speaking and counseling and inspiring. You have got to be joking!"

Sol did the work. He kept at it all alone for a year. Then one day as he sat in the chapel study, a light came on in his head. A voice within said: "Why not? He believed in you. You are starting to believe in yourself. God must believe in you, or He would not have put you here. Therefore, go for it."

Sol went home and told his mother, "I am going to become a rabbi." He found a way to enlist, even though most candidates start at eight years of age. The seminary changed its tactics for him. He has now been ordained for thirty years and currently serves as chief of chaplains for the Los Angeles City Police Department. He is a magnificent, inspiring, learned speaker.

Rabbi Sol Rothstein says, "I believe with all my heart that God's hand moves us through life. There is a design to our existence."

His favorite quotation is: "Hope in the Lord. Let your heart take courage. Yea, hope in the Lord."

Gary K. Yamamoto

Gary is an American who was born in Hawaii. He is an engineer whose career has taken him to most of the countries of the Far East and South Pacific. He speaks worldwide on the subjects of accountability, mastering change, stress management and creative problem-solving. He serves on the faculties of the University of Arizona and Pima College and is the author of several fine books and audio programs.

However, the part of his life which makes Gary most unusual is that he is a priest of the American Catholic Church, Malebar Rites. This spiritual background gives everything he does a loving and mystical aura. He is an excellent speaker who is in much demand in his field.

When I asked Gary which speaker had fired his heart and mind, this is what he told me: "I was inspired by a

Bob Montgomery
World famous speaker/author:
Memory, Listening

great speaker who grabbed my heart and never let go: W Mitchell. (See story in this book.) The two accidents that left him badly burned and confined to a wheelchair would have been enough to stop most people. But not Mitchell. As I listened to him speak, I was totally enthralled by his professional delivery and presence. I was struck by his famous words, "It's not what happens to you, it's what you do about it!" Those words have never stopped motivating me.

Each time I step onto the platform, I am thankful that I do not have the challenges that Mitchell has. When I think of how well he does, despite all that he has overcome, I feel privileged to be able to address an audience. I do my best, with my whole heart, to motivate them to rise to their highest levels of professional performance and personal enjoyment."

Gary told me that a quote by Rabindranath Tagore has had a great impact on him: "The song I have come to sing remains unsung. I have spent my time stringing and unstringing my instrument."

Gary explained, "I had acquired a tremendous amount of knowledge and great experiences which I intended to share with the world 'one of these days.' You see, I always felt that I was not quite ready.

"Tagore's quote made me realize that unless I did something, and soon, it could be *my* song or dream that would never be sung. It motivated me to get out of my limited mind-set and to share my message through speech, seminars, books, and tapes."

Robert Montgomery

Coming from the world of radio and television, Bob Montgomery is well known as the voice of "The Christophers Show." You might recall his opening line about "If we will each light one candle in the darkness... " Bob is a spiritual man who practices love in all that he creates.

Bob studied communication arts at Notre Dame, Catholic University in Washington, D.C., the University of Wisconsin, and Pace University, New York. He has

Norm Rebin
Top Canadian inspirational speaker/author,
trainer, Canadian government officials

earned numerous awards for his speaking and teaching skills, journalistic excellence, and service to youth.

He has taught more than 500,000 people during his thirty-year speaking, training, and consulting career. His audio albums are featured by Reader's Digest and Publishers Clearing House in the United States and Britain. Bob is the author of A *Master Guide to Public Speaking* (Harper & Row).

When you have the privilege of being a friend of such a great man and his lovely family it is delightful to ask which speaker inspired him most. Here is what he told me: "Dottie, the greatest speaker I ever heard in all of my career was Dr. Kenneth McFarland. He was asked this question from the audience: Can you state in one word what quality is most to be desired in public speaking?

"Dr. McFarland immediately responded, 'Vitality! Vitality of voice, of posture and of spirit. Vitality is the only world I know that embodies most of what is desired in the speaker, the content of the speech, and the delivery. Vitality is the characteristic that distinguishes the living from the non-living.'"

Bob Montgomery's favorite quote occurred when he heard Dr. Norman Vincent Peale quote Winston Churchill: "Never give up! Never, never, never, never, NEVER!"

Norman Rebin

The first time I saw this tall, impressive Canadian speaker, I knew there was something profound and unusual about him. He is a cousin of Tolstoy, with a unique blend of philosophy and pragmatic "on-line" business experience. As I listened to his tremendous program, I noticed that he mentioned my favorite "friends of the mind."

Norm Rebin has that magical quality of speaking directly to each heart in the room, until you feel that his words are a silver thread pulling you upward to the sunny room which contains his thoughts.

Norm told me his favorite quotation is this: "There are no bad or ugly kids. All a bad kid is, is a good kid waiting to come out." —Monsignor Pere Murray, Founder of Notre Dame College, Wilcox Saskatchewan, Canada.

Norm explains that this Canadian school insists that every one of its students participate or cheer on the teams at all events, from hockey to debating. The students also assist in the maintenance of the school. From this college, in a town whose population drops to less than one hundred souls during school breaks, have come an incredible percentage of the Canadian business, governmental, and organizational leaders in the past six decades.

Great speakers who inspire Norm Rebin are: the Russian speaker Doukhobor, survivor of the 'purges,' who told an American audience: "There is no freedom unless one learns to love again. Love is forgiveness. Without forgiveness, there can be no freedom and therefore, no future."

Norm's adopted American brother, E. Larry Moles, said, "All EGO is Easing God Out." Norm commented, "We need to remember, when we are so dazzled by our own talents, we begin to quote ourselves as we worship at the shrine of self."

As a child, Norm Rebin was taken by his Russian-speaking grandfather Efim to hear John G. Diefenbaker, then defense lawyer and later Canadian Prime Minister, who brought forth Canada's first Bill of Human Rights.

Norm told me: "His eloquence combined with his incisive logic set a pattern for me which dictated that no matter how passionately I speak, I must always have something worth saying.

"Later, as part of the Tuxis Parliament (student legislature for a day), I was captivated by Tommy Douglas, Saskatchewan Premier, who introduced Medicare to North America. He was a giant among orators.

"Tommy painted word pictures of people and situations recognizable by each person in the audience and combined them with pungent political salvos. All was underwritten with his deep belief in people and his commitment to them. Tommy said, 'In my speeches I drive every point home with humor. If people remember the joke, they'll remember my point.'

"This feisty little political pioneer showed me something important through his love for his audiences and their response to him on the platform and at the polls. I learned that flowery phrases alone mean little in grabbing, holding, and altering peoples emotions and actions. You must touch your audiences with your dreams and your passion... for them."

Benjamin Franklin

I hope you have enjoyed meeting these great speakers I know and love. There are many more, of course. It has been hard to choose.

To close this book I have a bit more to tell you about the speaker who has been the greatest influence in my life. I look at his big picture here in my office as I keyboard this manuscript. However, he is a speaker I have only heard in my mind and heart. No matter. Those are the two most important places to hear and understand any speaker.

Will Rogers is famous for saying that he never met a man he didn't like. This speaker never met anybody he didn't learn from and find fascinating. All the ladies of his day adored him. We still do.

He is Benjamin Franklin, newspaperman, printer, writer, diplomat, humorist, inventor, scientist, strategist, statesman, humanitarian, publisher, patriot, entrepreneur, Indian rights upholder, abolitionist, optometrist, postmaster, engineer, dreamer, doer, Freemason, leader— so many more titles. All of them together are not enough to describe his genius.

I love his following line: "Genius without education is like silver hidden in the deep blue depths of a mine."

If you are meeting my dear friend here for the first time, I am so glad to introduce you! Go and get his autobiography and fall in love with him too. There is plenty of him to go around. Ben does not believe in limitations.

This is the story I want to leave with you. Benjamin Franklin gathered his friends around him in Philadelphia and proposed that they build an auditorium. He said: "The purpose of the new building is to provide a platform and a warm welcome to speakers with ideas. No one will ever be turned away. They will find an eager audience here with us. We will listen to their ideas, no matter what the speakers' race, sex, religion, or what country they come from."

A revolutionary idea! Ben accomplished this dream. He did not wait for someone else to do it. He knew that making great things happen begins at home. Right where you are. He also knew that good ideas grow and expand until the light of them illumines all of the earth.

He fervently believed in freedom of speech and democracy. Ben persuaded Thomas Paine, the English speaker and author, to come to America to help with our great leap to freedom. Tom not only did so, he donated all the proceeds from his book, *The Age of Reason,* to General George Washington and his troops. Tom's book was our new country's first best-seller, even surpassing Ben's own annual editions of *Poor Richard's Almanac.*

Ben said that his greatest dream was that he himself could speak anywhere, with perfect freedom. So much so, that when he put his foot down to the ground of any country on earth he could say, "I am at home. This is my country."

And then my dear friend of the mind told me, "Dottie, I also wish that when I speak anywhere on earth, I can also say, 'These people are my people, my friends of the mind.'"

We hear you, Ben. We hear you.

Ben Franklin: My Love
by Dottie Walters

They laughed and derided,
"Go fly a kite, Ben!
But Ben just kept smiling;
A wise man. Ye ken?

He reached to the lightning
and tamed that wild beast.
He charted the oceans!
Ben's thoughts are like yeast.

Wherever he traveled
Minds Western or East,

Inquiring and learning,
exchanging a feast.

Of the new ways to do things
with freedom and song!
I long for this friendship,
I yearn to belong,

To Ben's merry comp'ny
When my life is frightful,
Then I read his stories.
His spirit delightful!

He sends hopes like kites up
"With teamwork, we CAN!
There's naught who can stop us...
Come, here is a plan!"

Ben opens the floodgates
of genius for me;
inventor and statesman
with bright strategy.

His favorite expression
of all I have read:
"Now, let's do the business!
Come! Just use your head."

Adored by the ladies?
They loved him. Their "Sun!"
(Now, need I inform you,
this lady is one?)

(Benjamin Franklin
American Diplomat, signer Declaration
of Independence, author, humorist, first U.S.
Postmaster General)

Index of Great Speakers